DIANE SEED'S
TOP 100
MEDITERRANEAN
DISHES

DIANE SEED'S TOP 100 MEDITERRANEAN DISHES

Illustrations by Sarah Hocombe

LONDON   NEW YORK   SYDNEY   TORONTO

Note on the recipes

The quantities given are for six people.

Recipes suitable for vegetarians (not including desserts) are marked with a (V) symbol. Please note that these recipes may include cheese and other dairy products.

For Maureen Green

Acknowledgements

I would like to thank Dr Antonio Capalbi who has shared my travels, and the subsequent cooking and eating. I would also like to thank the international students at St George's English School in Rome who, for many years, fed my imagination when they talked of home. Their parents cooked for me and explained their favourite recipes with skill and patience.

Sarah Hocombe's illustrations are even more than I hoped for, and they capture the many moods of this 'wine dark sea'. I am so happy to work with her.

This edition published 1994
by BCA by arrangement with BBC Books,
a division of BBC Enterprises Limited,
Woodlands, 80 Wood Lane,
London W12 0TT
First published 1994
© Diane Seed 1994

CN 2740

Designed by Isobel Gillan with Sarah Hocombe
Illustrations © Sarah Hocombe
Set in Granjon by Selwood Systems, Midsomer Norton
Printed and bound in Hong Kong by Mandarin Offset
Colour separation by Dot Gradations Ltd, near Chelmsford

CONTENTS

INTRODUCTION

Fifteen countries and three continents encompass this shallow land-locked sea, and the Mediterranean was the navel of the civilized world until Christopher Columbus and other great sailors opened up the trade routes to the Americas.

The Greeks, Phoenicians and Romans had colonized the whole area centuries before Christ, establishing an agriculture based on wheat, olives and wine, and in later years cargo ships zigzagging across the sea produced a constant cross-culture, so that variations on the same culinary theme are found from the Pillars of Hercules in the west to the cedars of Lebanon in the east. All the area enjoyed the same hot dry summers and wet warm winters so that crops migrated quite happily, and marauding pirates, invaders and seamen played their part in spreading new ingredients and recipes. The rise of Islam added a touch of spice to the Mediterranean daily fare, and expanded the cooking techniques.

In the past the Mediterranean people knew great hardship, struggling with constant volcanic activity, adverse weather conditions and a capricious sea. Foreign domination often caused crushing poverty and hunger was a constant enemy. This made survival itself seem a victory, and every meal became a cause for celebration. Today food is prepared with love and imagination, and every humble herb or vegetable is prized for its savour. We all enjoy Mediterranean cooking, and bask in the lazy pleasures of a cuisine dominated by the sun and sea. With its intense flavours, vibrant colours, and tantalizing aromas the food appeals to our senses. Mediterranean food is not artificial, contrived or affected; it depends for its effect on using one or two perfectly fresh, seasonal ingredients, chosen with care and prepared with love. It is family cooking at its best, and its appeal is universal.

Fresh herbs such as oregano, basil, mint, parsley, and dill are used with flair and imagination to bring the simple ingredients to life. Fennel gives an inimitable tang to pork and fish, while rocket adds a pungent quality to many Italian and Turkish dishes. Every region has its favourite herb combination, ranging from the Provençal bouquet garni to the Ligurian 'preboggion'. Today, when many people no longer have a kitchen garden, market stalls specialize in fresh herbs, and in Italy a small bunch of *odori* – onion, celery and carrot – are tucked, free of charge, into the shopping bag when you purchase any fruit or vegetables. Many of the most aromatic herbs grow wild, and in summer a warm, oregano-scented breeze wafts down from the Greek hills. These wild herbs have more flavour than the cultivated variety, and even today in many countries you see the local women scouring the countryside for wild herbs and salad leaves. Saffron adds fragrance and colour to many dishes, and the Arabic influence is seen in the recipes using cinnamon, cumin and coriander.

The Roman soldiers' love of garlic was legendary. *Ubi Roma ibi allium.* They carried it to the most far-flung corners of the Empire, and today to many people garlic is synonymous with Mediterranean cooking. Nobody who has eaten a slice of Italian *bruschetta* will forget how good a simple piece of coarse bread can taste when it is anointed with good olive oil and rubbed vigorously with garlic, and some of the very best pasta sauces start with the masterly combination of *aglio, olio e peperoncino* (garlic, olive oil and chilli pepper). Dried beans, peas and chick peas (garbanzos) are transformed into irresistible dishes, and Esau, in the Old Testament, was lured into renouncing his birthright for a lentil and garlic stew.

During the Renaissance Lorenzo the Magnificent's emissary to Naples described the people there as *mangiafoglie*, or leaf eaters. This epithet could still be applied to most of the Mediterranean people. Fresh, seasonal vegetables are so important they are served as a dish in their own right, and frozen-food manufacturers have a hard time competing with the street markets, where the produce has been freshly picked, carefully washed and lovingly arranged. The Arabs introduced Europe to the aubergine (eggplant) and Turkey and Sicily have a seemingly endless repertoire of recipes for this. Italy and Provence rely heavily on courgettes (zucchini), and the ubiquitous artichoke is one of my favourite vegetables.

Good, crusty, freshly-baked bread is an important ingredient and treated with due respect. If a piece of bread falls to the floor it will be carefully retrieved and set to one side so that it is never trodden into the ground.

Citrus fruits, melons, figs, pomegranates, quinces and prickly pears conjure up the Mediterranean, yet many of these fruits originally came from Persia via Turkey. They were prized for their sweet, refreshing juices and today no meal is complete without a luscious bowl of fruit. The harem in Topkapi Palace epitomizes opulent pleasures, and one of the most beautiful rooms is the fruit room, completely walled with ceramic tiles decorated with fruit designs.

In the Mediterranean wine is an everyday accompaniment to meals, and one might even classify it as 'an essential ingredient'. The Persian poet Omar Khayyam considered life's necessities to be 'a jug of wine, a loaf of bread, and Thou'. It amuses me to reflect that had he lived a little further north his beloved would undoubtedly have been even further down the list, to make place for the olive. The olive appears on its own at breakfast, lunch and dinner, and it is used in countless recipes combined with meat, fish, poultry, bread and rice. In hard times bread and olives often provided a complete meal, and today, when things are easier, it would be difficult to find a Mediterranean home without several types of olives in the larder. The same is true of olive oil.

Olive oil is the traditional cooking oil used in Mediterranean countries. In the past, when many families kept a pig, home-produced lard was used in some western countries to help the family budget, but once the pig disappeared from most backyards, olive oil replaced lard in many recipes. Today, more and more people in non-Mediterranean countries are beginning to use olive oil, hoping to recapture the tantalizing flavours of meals enjoyed in sunny climes. Nutritionists and doctors have added their voice, too, extolling the healthy eating patterns of the Mediterranean, where death from coronary disease is rarer, thanks to a diet low in animal fats.

Extra-virgin olive oil is the best quality olive oil. It has a very good flavour, and by law its acidity content is less than 1 per cent. This is the one to choose when you want to add a fine thread of raw olive oil to garnish a cooked dish. It will add a superb final touch to pulses, vegetables, soups, fish and salads. In this category there are many fine oils and the taste differs according to the soil and climate of the area where it is produced. You need to taste several to choose the oil that appeals most to you, and there is no right answer.

Fine virgin olive oil is a very good quality oil, with less than 1.5 per cent acidity content. It can be used in the same way as the extra-virgin olive oil.

Semi-fine or ordinary virgin olive oil has a maximum acidity of 3 per cent and can be used for any cooked dish. I like this quality oil for frying since it responds well to high cooking temperatures and the anti-oxidants and mono-unsaturated fatty acids mean the filtered oil can be re-used quite safely two or three times for the same kind of food. This helps to off-set the expense of deep-frying in olive oil.

In this collection of recipes I have chosen my own personal favourites, so I have included some pasta recipes from my other books. This has been kept to a very few instances, however, and since all cooking is creative and constantly changing, I am sure my way of cooking them has changed over the years.

SOUPS

In the past, when many of the Mediterranean countries were very poor, soups were often a one-course complete meal, served with a great quantity of bread, to provide warmth, comfort and nourishment during the colder months. These hearty, robust soups usually contained lentils, chick peas (garbanzos) or beans, which were known as 'the poor man's meat'. Pulses were used as well in the 'lean' days decreed by the Church, and in Muslim countries today the Ramadan fast is still usually broken with a nourishing soup. Fresh vegetables are used in season, and eggs are often added to provide more nourishment.

Many of the great Mediterranean fish soups are one-course complete meals even in the more affluent modern times, and a few pieces of toasted bread or boiled potatoes are all that are needed to complete the feast. Every coastal region has its own speciality, and since the sea is always capricious the ingredients vary according to the catch. In the past many of these soups were made by local fishermen with the fish that did not command high prices in the market. They ate the fish that had no commercial value, in the same way as the butchers in the old Roman slaughterhouse were paid with the *quinto quarto* or fifth quarter of the animal, the part that could not be sold, like the head, trotters and innards. The tendency today to add lobster and prime-quality fish is a distortion of a dish that originated in the *cucina povera* tradition. In the south of Spain there are the gazpacho-type cold soups, but in the rest of the Mediterranean there is no traditional equivalent.

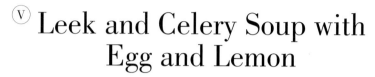

ⓥ Leek and Celery Soup with Egg and Lemon

The Greek combination of egg and lemon – avgolémono – enhances chicken, fish, meatballs and soups. In this recipe it gives the soup a creamy texture with a refreshingly tart flavour.

750 g (1½ lb) leeks, chopped
4 celery stalks, chopped
2 tablespoons extra-virgin olive oil
750 ml (1¼ pints) light stock
juice of 1 lemon
2 eggs
salt and freshly ground black pepper

Stew the leeks and celery gently in the olive oil until they are soft. Add the stock and simmer for 20 minutes. Purée the mixture. This stage can be prepared in advance.

When ready to serve beat together the lemon juice and eggs until light and frothy, and reheat the soup. Slowly beat a ladleful of hot soup into the egg and lemon mixture, then add this back to the rest of the soup, stirring well to make sure the eggs do not coagulate. Check the seasoning and serve.

Ⓥ Zuppa di Asparagi

CALABRIAN ASPARAGUS SOUP

The south of Italy has many recipes which include the thin wild asparagus that grows round the Mediterranean. In Calabria it can be bought at the market stalls, and this is a favourite spring soup. If you are in an extravagant mood, you can also make it with thin, cultivated green asparagus.

1.5 kg (3 lb) green asparagus
salt and freshly ground black pepper
3 tablespoons extra-virgin olive oil
1 clove garlic, finely chopped
6 eggs, beaten
3 tablespoons grated Pecorino or Parmesan cheese
6 round slices white bread, toasted

Discard the tough ends of the asparagus and chop the rest into 2.5 cm (1 in) lengths. Cook in boiling salted water. Heat the oil and add the garlic and drained asparagus. Grind on a little black pepper, then add 1.5 litres (2½ pints) boiling, lightly-salted water. Cook for another 3 minutes, then stir in the eggs and cheese. Stir for a few minutes until the eggs coagulate and form threads. Check the seasoning and serve with rounds of toast.

Ⓥ Soupe des Maures

PUMPKIN SOUP

Pumpkin and white beans are an interesting combination found in several Mediterranean countries. In the south of Italy the beans are served with puréed pumpkin as a substantial vegetable dish, while in France the beans are puréed with the pumpkin to make a thick soup.

100 g (4 oz) dried white beans (e.g. cannellini or butter beans) or
250 g (9 oz) can
2 tablespoons olive oil
2 leeks, sliced
$\frac{1}{2}$ celery stalk, sliced
350 g (12 oz) pumpkin
1.5 litres ($2\frac{1}{2}$ pints) light stock
salt and freshly ground black pepper

If using dried beans soak them for 10 hours. Drain and rinse the beans. Boil slowly in water to cover for about $1\frac{1}{2}$ hours or until soft, then drain.

Heat the oil and gently cook the leeks and celery until the leeks are soft. Peel the pumpkin, remove the seeds and chop the flesh into small pieces. Add the pumpkin to the pan and cook gently for a few minutes before adding the drained cooked or canned beans and half the stock. Cook until the pumpkin is tender, then purée with the rest of the stock. Season to taste.

Ⓥ Potaje de Espinacas y Garbanzos

SPINACH AND CHICK PEA SOUP

This is a wonderful combination that used to be eaten during Lent, when the Church decreed a meatless diet. Today, in a more relaxed era, this thick broth is enjoyed for its flavour, and the same mixture is often reduced and served as a thick dip for tapas.

300 g (11 oz) chick peas (garbanzos)
1 bay leaf
1 small or $\frac{1}{2}$ large head garlic
1 large onion, peeled and quartered
500 g (1 lb 2 oz) spinach leaves, washed
salt and either cayenne or freshly ground black pepper
2 tablespoons extra-virgin olive oil
2 cloves garlic, chopped
1 thick slice stale white bread, crumbled
2 tablespoons chopped fresh parsley
1 teaspoon ground cumin (optional)

Soak the chick peas (garbanzos) overnight in cold water. Drain and place in a pan with enough cold water to cover. Add the bay leaf, the unpeeled garlic and the onion. Bring to the boil, cover and simmer for about 1 hour until the chick peas are tender.

Cook the spinach in a separate pan, using just the water trapped in the leaves after washing, with a little added salt. Drain and reserve.

Heat the oil and gently fry the 2 cloves of chopped garlic with the bread and parsley. Remove and blend to a smooth paste with a little of the chick pea cooking water.

Remove and discard the head of garlic, bay leaf and onion segments cooked with the chick peas. Stir in the spinach and gradually mix in the garlic and bread paste. Cover and simmer for 10 minutes. Season to taste with cumin (if using), salt and pepper and serve.

ⓥ Zuppa di Zucchine

COURGETTE SOUP

This lovely Neapolitan speciality comes from the same tradition as the Spaghetti with Courgettes (Zucchini) recipe (see page 32). I remember eating it for the first time in Amalfi on a terrace shaded by fragrant lemon trees, and it seemed to me that this pale yellow and green summer soup reflected the colours of the great dimpled Amalfi lemons with their bright green leaves.

1 kg (2 lb) courgettes (zucchini)
4 tablespoons extra-virgin olive oil
1.5 litres (2½ pints) vegetable stock or water
salt and freshly ground black pepper
3 eggs
3 tablespoons freshly grated Parmesan cheese
1 tablespoon chopped fresh parsley
12 fresh basil leaves, roughly chopped
6 rounds bread, toasted

Without peeling the courgettes, cut them into small cubes. Heat the oil and cook the courgettes for 5 minutes, stirring continuously. Add the boiling vegetable stock or water, season to taste, cover and stew gently for 20 minutes. Beat the eggs and cheese together with the parsley and basil leaves.

Just before serving put the toast in a soup tureen. Remove the soup from the heat and quickly stir in the egg mixture. Pour over the toast, add a little more freshly ground black pepper and serve at once.

Zuppa di Fagioli

BEAN SOUP

This hearty soup exists in many versions, and it was often eaten as a complete one-dish meal. Occasionally a few shellfish were added to make a richer dish, and pulses and frutti di mare *are a delicious combination found along all the Italian coastline.*

350 g (12 oz) dried borlotti beans
2 tablespoons olive oil
1 small hot chilli pepper, de-seeded and finely chopped
1 carrot, finely chopped
2 leeks, finely chopped
1 onion, finely chopped
1 celery stalk, finely chopped
2 cloves garlic, finely chopped
1 sprig fresh rosemary
1 ham bone (optional)
salt and freshly ground black pepper
1 tablespoon very good quality extra-virgin olive oil to 'dress' the soup
(optional)

Put the beans to soak, covered with plenty of cold water, for 12 hours. Rinse and drain.

Heat the oil and add the chilli, vegetables and rosemary. When they begin to change colour add the drained beans and ham bone if desired. Cover with cold water and cook slowly for 2 hours. Remove the chilli and bone, and purée half the mixture. Stir the purée back into the remaining beans, check the seasoning and re-heat before serving.

It is customary to pour a fine thread of very good extra-virgin olive oil on top of each serving.

(V) Zuppa di Funghi

WILD MUSHROOM SOUP

Wild mushrooms from the great forests of the Sila in Calabria have always enriched the regional dishes, and you often come across a lively, spur-of-the-moment market, as the local men trade their wares from the backs of their cars, swapping among themselves to get greater variety, and selling some of their prizes to passing motorists. If you do not have wild mushrooms you can use a small packet of dried ceps to give extra flavour to cultivated large flat mushrooms. It is not worth making this soup with button mushrooms alone.

1 kg (2 lb) mixed wild mushrooms
salt and freshly ground black pepper
1 tablespoon olive oil
25 g (1 oz) fatty bacon, chopped (optional)
2 cloves garlic, chopped
1 medium onion, finely sliced
1 litre ($1\frac{3}{4}$ pints) vegetable or light meat stock
1 tablespoon fresh tomato sauce (see page 38)
100 g (4 oz) Parmesan or Pecorino cheese, freshly grated
50 g (2 oz) chopped fresh parsley

Wipe the mushrooms clean with a damp sponge, dry, then slice finely and leave covered with salt in a colander for 2 to 3 hours. Rinse and leave to drain. If using dried ceps, soak in a little warm water for 15 minutes.

Heat the oil and gently fry the bacon (if using), garlic and onion until almost transparent. Heat the stock and stir in the dried ceps, if using, with their strained liquid. Stir in the tomato sauce and mushrooms and cook in the stock for 20 minutes.

When ready to serve, stir in the cheese, check the seasoning and sprinkle the parsley on top.

Caldo de Perro

CÁDIZ FISH SOUP

This soup comes from the small port of El Puerto de Santa Maria, near Cádiz in Spain. Unlike many of the more substantial complete-meal Mediterranean fish soups, it really is a 'first course' dish, and it gets its inimitable flavour from the unexpected addition of bitter Seville orange juice.

1 kg (2 lb) very fresh small hake, cod or whiting, thickly sliced
coarse salt and freshly ground black pepper
6 tablespoons extra-virgin olive oil
3 cloves garlic, peeled
1 large onion, finely chopped
1.5 litres (2½ pints) fish stock or water
juice of 2 Seville oranges or juice of 1 sweet orange and 1 lemon

Cover the fish slices with coarse salt and leave for 1 hour. Remove the slices of fish, rinse, drain and put on one side.

Heat the oil and cook the whole garlic cloves until they turn golden brown. Discard the garlic, add the onion and cook gently until soft. Pour in half the stock or water, simmer for 15 minutes, then add the fish and the rest of the stock. Cover and cook gently for another 10 minutes. At the end of this time lift out the fish with a slotted spoon and remove and discard the bones and skin. Break the fish into bite-sized pieces and return to the soup with the orange juice. Leave the soup to stand for 10 minutes so the flavours amalgamate, then add pepper to taste and re-heat and serve hot.

Aigo-Sau

MONKFISH SOUP

Provence has given us majestic, world-famous fish soups like
bouillabaisse *and* bourride, *but also some good simple soups that*
are less daunting and more easily prepared with fish that are not
from the Mediterranean. For this recipe any white fish can be used
if you do not have monkfish. This soup is usually served with the
broth as a first course, and with the fish and potatoes as a main
course. This belongs to the frugal Mediterranean tradition where,
in the past, such a dish could be stretched to provide two meals.

1.5 kg (3 lb) monkfish or other white fish
6 potatoes, peeled and thinly sliced
1 large onion, finely chopped
3 cloves garlic, finely chopped
2 very ripe tomatoes, peeled
1 bouquet garni of thyme, bay leaf, fennel and parsley
zest or dried peel of 1 orange
salt and freshly ground black pepper
4 tablespoons extra-virgin olive oil
6 rounds bread, toasted

Cut the fish into cutlets or fillets. In a large pan put the fish and
all the vegetables, herbs, orange zest or dried orange peel and
seasoning. Pour on the oil and leave to marinate for 30 minutes.
At the end of this time cover with water and bring to the boil.
Lower the heat, cover and cook gently for 10 minutes. Then
check the seasoning, and remove the bouquet garni.

If desired, the rounds of toast can be rubbed with garlic and
olive oil. Serve the broth poured over the toast, and the fish and
potatoes on a separate plate, either at the same time or as a
second course.

Zuppa di Lattuga e Frutti di Mare

LETTUCE AND SHELLFISH SOUP

I love this elegant soup and often serve it as an easy starter for summer dinner parties.

750 g ($1\frac{1}{2}$ lb) clams
750 g ($1\frac{1}{2}$ lb) mussels
5 scallops
salt and freshly ground black pepper
1 tablespoon lemon juice
4 tablespoons extra-virgin olive oil
2 cloves garlic, finely chopped
2 shallots, finely chopped
300 g (11 oz) potatoes, peeled and sliced
300 g (11 oz) lettuce leaves

Scrub the clams and mussels, then put with 250 ml (8 fl oz) water in a covered pan and boil quickly until the shells open. Discard any that do not open. Strain the cooking liquid and reserve. Remove the mussels and clams from their shells and chop them unless they are already very small. Gently cook the scallops for 3 minutes in the water from the mussels and clams. Lift out with a slotted spoon and cut into small pieces. Reserve the water. Season the shellfish and squeeze on a little lemon juice.

Heat half the oil and gently cook the garlic and shallots until soft. Add the potatoes, the shellfish water and 500 ml (17 fl oz) boiling water. Season, cover and simmer for 20 minutes. When the potatoes are soft, purée the mixture together with the roughly chopped lettuce leaves. Check the seasoning.

Ladle a little soup into individual bowls, arrange the shellfish on top and pour on a fine thread of olive oil.

Zuppa di Pesce

MEDITERRANEAN FISH SOUP FROM PUGLIA

Italy has a long coastline and every region has its special fish soup. This soup from Puglia is a meal in itself and needs to be treated as a main course. There is none of the mystique that the French seem to give to their great fish soups, but the fish must be fresh and several different types should be used. Traditionally, these dishes were cooked with the less valuable fish since the fishermen sold the best of their catch and ate what was left. Today, in the over-fished Mediterranean, all fresh fish is valuable, but fish soup is still made from the smaller fish that feed on the rocks as these have more flavour than the larger varieties. People seem to be philosophical about the bones. I cook the whole fish in the soup, but lift it out and fillet it before serving with the soup.

750 g ($1\frac{1}{2}$ lb) mixed shellfish, e.g. mussels, squid, cuttlefish, prawns (shrimps)
1.25 kg ($2\frac{1}{2}$ lb) assorted fish, e.g. mullet, scorpion fish (rascasse), grouper
4 tablespoons extra-virgin olive oil
1 onion, chopped
2 cloves garlic, chopped
1 celery stalk, finely chopped
500 g (1lb 2 oz) Italian plum tomatoes, peeled and chopped
1 tablespoon chopped fresh parsley
salt and freshly ground black pepper

Scrub the mussels, cook for a few minutes in a little boiling water and discard any that fail to open. Remove them from the liquid and drain. Break off and discard half of each shell, keeping the half to which the mussel is attached. Reserve the mussels.

Clean the remaining shellfish. Cut the cuttlefish and squid sacs into rings and the tentacles into segments. Gut and scale the fish but leave the heads intact.

Heat the oil and gently fry the onion and garlic until they begin to change colour. Add the celery, tomatoes with their juice, parsley and seasoning. Cook gently until the celery is very soft, then add the cuttlefish and squid. After 10 minutes put in the whole fish. Cover and stew gently for 15 minutes. Remove the whole fish with a slotted spoon and fillet them. Add the mussels and shelled prawns and cook for 5 minutes, then return the filleted fish to the soup. To avoid breaking up the fish do not stir again. Serve at once. It is usual to serve with some small rounds of toasted bread as a main course.

BREAD, PASTA AND RICE

THE ROMANS BUILT
huge beehive-shaped bread ovens in every country they conquered, and the Roman roads spread everywhere around the Mediterranean. The baker's oven became the focal point of village life, even acting as a communal kitchen, as the women brought in their individual casseroles to enjoy long slow cooking in the embers of the bread oven when the day's baking was done. Even today, when life is easier, bread still has an almost religious significance, and in parts of Sicily and Greece I have seen bread that has accidentally fallen on the floor being carefully retrieved and kissed with reverence, before being set aside.

The same good wheat is used in Italy to make pasta. In the south some traditional *casareccia* pasta is made at home with a flour-and-water dough. This rustic pasta is usually rather thick and substantial and bears no resemblance to the thin, light egg pasta made in Emilia Romagna. The true Mediterranean pasta is made with durum wheat and this pasta needs to be worked with industrial machines. Traditionally packets of dried pasta are used, and spaghetti is not made at home. For the olive oil-based pasta sauces that are so typical of the Mediterranean it is best to use good Italian dried pasta. In other areas rice replaces wheat as the staple diet, and vegetables and seafood are used in small quantities to provide endless variety. Cracked wheat is popular in the eastern Mediterranean, and many countries have a thin, paper-like pastry that can be used like the Greek filo leaves.

Ⓥ Olive Bread

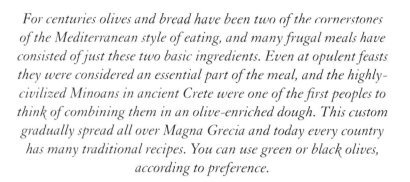

*For centuries olives and bread have been two of the cornerstones
of the Mediterranean style of eating, and many frugal meals have
consisted of just these two basic ingredients. Even at opulent feasts
they were considered an essential part of the meal, and the highly-
civilized Minoans in ancient Crete were one of the first peoples to
think of combining them in an olive-enriched dough. This custom
gradually spread all over Magna Grecia and today every country
has many traditional recipes. You can use green or black olives,
according to preference.*

250 g (9 oz) plain (all-purpose) white flour
250 g (9 oz) wholewheat flour
50 g (2 oz) dried yeast
1 teaspoon salt
6 tablespoons extra-virgin olive oil
200 g (7 oz) onions, finely chopped
100 g (4 oz) stoned olives, chopped
1 tablespoon chopped fresh rosemary
olive oil for brushing the loaf

Mix the two flours together and dissolve the yeast in a little
tepid water. Put half the flour in a bowl, add the salt, make a
well in the middle and pour in the yeast mixture, 3 tablespoons
olive oil and 250 ml (8 fl oz) tepid water. Knead by hand for
about 15 minutes, or use a food processor to speed up the
process, gradually working in as much of the remaining flour
as needed to make a firm elastic dough. Cover and leave in a
warm place until the dough has risen to twice its original size.

Heat the remaining olive oil in a pan and gently cook the
onions until soft. Add the olives and rosemary, then work them
into the dough and continue kneading for another few minutes.
Divide the dough into 2 round, flat loaves, set on an oiled
baking tray, cover with a cloth, and leave in a warm place for
another hour. At the end of this time pre-heat the oven to
190°C, 375°F (Gas Mark 5).

Brush the bread with olive oil and bake in the oven for about
25 minutes. The loaf should be golden brown and sound hollow
when tapped on the bottom.

ⓥ Manaiesh bi Zahtar

LEBANESE BREAD

These small breads are easy to make and they do not need too much time to rise. The traditional zahtar can be purchased at Middle Eastern speciality shops and is a mixture of thyme, sesame seeds, summer savory and sumac (found in Middle Eastern stores). If you can't find traditional zahtar you can improvize with your own herb topping.

15 g ($\frac{1}{2}$ oz) fresh yeast
1 egg, beaten
7 tablespoons olive oil
2 tablespoons sugar
2 teaspoons salt
450 g (1 lb) plain (all-purpose) white flour
3 tablespoons zahtar, or herbs of your choice

Dissolve the yeast in 3 tablespoons tepid water, then add the egg, 4 tablespoons of the olive oil and the sugar. Add the salt to the flour, then gradually stir in the yeast mixture and enough tepid water to make a stiff dough. Depending on the flour used you will need about 300 ml (10 fl oz) tepid water. Knead until you have a smooth elastic dough. Put in a roomy, oiled plastic bag and set to rise in a warm, draught-proof place for about 45 minutes. Pre-heat the oven to 230°C, 450°F (Gas Mark 8).

Divide the dough into 6 pieces. On a floured board roll out each ball to form an oblong about 1 cm ($\frac{1}{2}$ in) high. Arrange on an oiled baking sheet, cover with cling-film and leave for 15 minutes.

Mix together the zahtar and remaining olive oil. Brush evenly over each bread, pressing in your fingers to make a dimpled pattern. Bake in the hot oven for 10 minutes, then wrap in a cloth and serve hot.

Ⓥ Pizza Margherita

When Italy became a united nation in 1870, a Neapolitan pizzaiolo, in a burst of patriotic fervour, named this tomato, basil and Mozzarella pizza, which bore the colours of the new tricolour flag, 'Margherita', after the Queen, who was said to be particularly fond of this variation. The pizza pan should be very thick to avoid the bottom burning, and a heavy rectangular pan is preferable to a thin round tray. The quantities given will serve four as a starter. Small individual pizzette can be made for party nibbles, using a pastry cutter of the desired diameter before adding the topping.

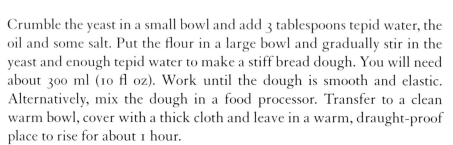

Dough
25 g (1 oz) fresh yeast
1 tablespoon extra-virgin olive oil
salt
500 g (1 lb 2 oz) plain (all-purpose) white flour

Topping
300 g (11 oz) Mozzarella cheese
500 g (1 lb 2 oz) ripe tomatoes
3 tablespoons extra-virgin olive oil
8 fresh basil leaves, cut into ribbons just before using
2 tablespoons freshly grated Parmesan cheese
salt

Crumble the yeast in a small bowl and add 3 tablespoons tepid water, the oil and some salt. Put the flour in a large bowl and gradually stir in the yeast and enough tepid water to make a stiff bread dough. You will need about 300 ml (10 fl oz). Work until the dough is smooth and elastic. Alternatively, mix the dough in a food processor. Transfer to a clean warm bowl, cover with a thick cloth and leave in a warm, draught-proof place to rise for about 1 hour.

If the Mozzarella is very fresh it is advisable to slice it in advance and place it on a paper towel so that the whey can be absorbed. Peel the tomatoes by plunging them into boiling water, cut into segments, removing the seeds, and place in a colander to drain.

Pre-heat the oven to 220°C, 425°F (Gas Mark 7) and lightly oil the tray for the pizza. Roll out the dough to make a thin supple sheet and place on the prepared baking tray. Brush the surface with oil, then cover the pizza with thin slices of Mozzarella. Scatter on the basil and Parmesan, then arrange flat fillets of tomato over the surface. Lightly salt the tomatoes and add a thin thread of oil. Put into the hot oven and bake for about 15 to 20 minutes. Half-way through the cooking it may be necessary to turn the pizza round so that it browns evenly.

Ⓥ Borek

FILO PASTRY STUFFED WITH CHEESE

Packets of filo pastry can be bought in most countries and the gossamer-thin sheets can be used in many ingenious ways. In Turkey the most common filling is Feta cheese and dill, and the filo is rolled into cigar shapes. Before you begin this recipe, taste the Feta cheese. If it is very salty, soak it in a little cold water overnight.

500 g (1 lb 2 oz) Feta cheese, soaked if necessary
2 eggs, beaten
4 tablespoons chopped fresh dill
salt and freshly ground black pepper
1 packet filo pastry
olive oil

Beat the cheese and eggs into a smooth paste. Stir in the dill, then season to taste.

Work with three sheets of filo at a time, keeping the other sheets in their original wrapping to prevent them drying out. Stack the three sheets of pastry one on top of each other, brushing each with olive oil before placing the next on top. Cut into rectangles measuring 13 × 20 cm (5 × 8 in). Place a thin cylinder of stuffing 9 cm ($3\frac{1}{2}$ in) long on the short side, fold over the long edges, then roll up to make a neat oblong. These borek are usually deep-fried but they can also be brushed with olive oil and cooked on a greased baking tray in a very hot oven at 220°C, 425°F (Gas Mark 7), until golden brown. They should be served hot.

 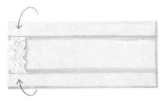

Pizzelle di Scàmmaro

PASTA WITH GREEN LEAF FILLING

This recipe is made with scarola *which, in English, is called Batavian endive and traditionally the dish was eaten on days such as Christmas Eve when the Church banned meat.* *You can substitute broccoli, spinach or any other tender green leaves.*

Dough
25 g (1 oz) fresh yeast
4 tablespoons extra-virgin olive oil
salt and freshly ground black pepper
500 g (1 lb 2 oz) plain (all-purpose) white flour

Filling
500 g (1 lb 2 oz) green leaves
salt
3 tablespoons olive oil
1 clove garlic, minced
3 anchovy fillets, chopped
1 teaspoon capers
200 g (7 oz) stoned black olives
1 tablespoon sultanas (white raisins)
oil for deep-frying

Make the dough in the same way as the recipe for Pizza Margherita (see page 28).

Cook the green leaves in boiling, salted water and drain carefully while they are still a good green colour. Heat the oil and gently fry the garlic and chopped anchovy until the garlic begins to turn a golden brown. Squeeze all the water from the greens, chop and add to the pan, stirring so that they become coated with the oil. Stir in the rinsed and dried capers, olives and the sultanas.

When the dough has risen, divide into 12 small balls, working one at a time. Roll out very thinly on a floured board and spoon a little filling into the middle. Fold over and seal the edges with a little water and light pressure. I usually make a half moon, and press a fork around the edges.

When all the *pizzelle* have been made, cover with a cloth. When ready to serve, heat the oil for deep-frying and fry the *pizzelle* until golden brown, then serve. It is important not to let them brown too quickly on the outside or the inside will still be cold. They must be eaten very hot.

ⓥ Focaccia con la Ricotta

FOCACCIA WITH RICOTTA CHEESE

Puglia, in the 'heel' of Italy, has some of the most interesting traditional recipes, using the high quality grain that supported the first small industrial pasta factories. It is important to simulate the effect of a stone, wood-fuelled oven, so the baking tin should be placed on a very hot stainless-steel baking sheet or solid oven shelf.

450 g (1 lb) ricotta cheese
40 g (1½ oz) fresh yeast
4 tablespoons extra-virgin olive oil
600 g (1 lb 5 oz) plain (all-purpose) white flour
3 eggs, beaten
250 g (9 oz) Mozzarella cheese, cubed
3 tablespoons freshly grated Parmesan cheese
¼ teaspoon ground nutmeg
salt and freshly ground black pepper
oil for greasing and brushing

Put the ricotta in a sieve for about 1 hour to strain off the excess liquid. Pre-heat the oven to 240°C, 475°F (Gas Mark 9).

Dissolve the yeast in 3 tablespoons tepid water then add the oil. Stir into the flour, adding about 300 ml (10 fl oz) tepid water to make a smooth, elastic dough when kneaded for about 10 minutes.

Mix the ricotta, the eggs, the Mozzarella and the Parmesan cheese together and stir in the nutmeg and seasoning. Lightly oil a round, shallow baking tin and roll out two-thirds of the dough to cover the base with about 3 cm (1¼ in) above the top of the tin. Roll out the remaining dough to a circle, a little larger in diameter than the tin.

Spread the cheese filling evenly over the base, then cover with the other circle of dough. Press the two edges together and roll over to form a border around the outside of the focaccia. Brush all the top with a little extra-virgin olive oil and bake for 30 minutes.

ⓥ Spaghetti alle Zucchine

SPAGHETTI WITH COURGETTES

This pasta recipe appears throughout southern Italy in various guises. It is quick, easy, healthy and delicious. If you feel like being more lavish, stir melted butter and grated Parmesan cheese into the pasta before adding the fried courgettes. This is the elaboration made famous along the Amalfi coast by the trattoria *Maria Grazia, in the village of Marina del Cantone.*

1 kg (2 lb) small courgettes (zucchini)
4 tablespoons olive oil
salt and freshly ground black pepper
2 tablespoons coarse salt
500 g (1 lb 2 oz) spaghetti
100 g (4 oz) Parmesan cheese, freshly grated (optional)
100 g (4 oz) butter, melted (optional)

Wash the courgettes but do not remove the skin. Dry and slice into thin discs. Heat the oil and gently cook the courgettes, stirring from time to time. Season with salt and freshly ground black pepper.

Bring 4 litres (7 pints) of water to the boil in a large, tall pan and add about 2 tablespoons coarse salt. When the water is boiling briskly, ease in the spaghetti and partly cover the pan so that the water returns to the boil as quickly as possible. Stir the pasta with a large fork so that it swirls about in the water. Try a strand of pasta every so often to see if it is cooked, and drain quickly while it is still *al dente*.

Turn the pasta into a large, heated serving bowl and stir in the courgettes and their oil. (It helps to have someone else adding the courgettes while you are lifting the pasta with a couple of forks.)

If you want to use the Maria Grazia version remove the courgettes from the pan with a slotted spoon and drain on paper towels to remove excess oil. Stir the freshly grated Parmesan cheese and melted butter into the pasta before adding the courgettes.

(V)

Trenette al Pesto

PASTA WITH BASIL SAUCE

In spring and summer all along the Italian Ligurian coast every window-sill, doorway and outside staircase are occupied by fragrant pots of basil, and the air is redolent with the perfume drifting up from all the containers, which range from old paint cans and saucepans to beautiful ceramic creations. Pesto sauce is made by pounding basil leaves with garlic, pine nuts and olive oil, and in the past Genoese sailors used to take supplies of this sauce on board their great sailing ships to provision their voyages of discovery. Traditionally the pounding was done by hand, using basil grown in the warm sea breezes. Today a food processor makes life much easier and, although purists may frown, I make this, my favourite sauce, in the time it takes for the pasta to cook. Today, even in Liguria, many people use Parmesan cheese in place of the more pungent Pecorino, and I follow their example.

150 g (5 oz) fresh basil leaves
50 g (2 oz) pine nuts or walnuts or blanched almonds
2 large cloves garlic, peeled
75 g (3 oz) Parmesan cheese, freshly grated
500 g (1 lb 2 oz) trenette, linguine or spaghetti
2 tablespoons coarse salt
salt and freshly ground black pepper
5 tablespoons extra-virgin olive oil

Remove the basil leaves from their stalks and wash gently. Do not wash under running water or you will bruise the leaves. Gently pat dry and put to one side. In a processor grind together the nuts, garlic and cheese.

Cook the pasta in 4 litres (7 pints) of boiling water to which you have added the coarse salt. Follow the packet directions carefully to avoid over-cooking. Ease the pasta into the water and half-cover the pan so that the water comes back to the boil as quickly as possible.

Now process the basil leaves, adding pepper, a little salt and the olive oil, pouring slowly with the machine running. You will add a tablespoon of the pasta cooking liquid to the sauce, so be careful not to put in too much salt at this stage. Drain the pasta, tip into a large heated serving bowl and gradually stir in the pesto, diluted with a little pasta water. Work quickly, lifting up the pasta with a large fork to make sure that every strand is coated with the pesto sauce. Serve at once.

ⓥ Linguine con Peperoni

LINGUINE WITH SWEET PEPPER SAUCE

Ripe red and yellow sweet peppers (capsicums) are needed for this recipe. The skins need to be removed, and the traditional way is to put them under a fierce grill (broiler) or on the naked flame of a gas burner. The skin needs to blacken and blister on all sides, and the peppers are afterwards put into in a paper or plastic bag and allowed to cool. The skin then comes off fairly easily. With this method the wonderful aroma of roasting peppers permeates the kitchen, but the gas stove is filthy and I usually burn my fingers in the process! When I am in a hurry I cook them with their skins and then pass the sauce through a food mill.

6 large red or yellow sweet peppers (capsicums), skinned
3 tablespoons olive oil
3 cloves garlic, chopped
1 onion, chopped
salt and freshly ground black pepper
2 tablespoons coarse salt
500 g (1 lb 2 oz) linguine
50 g (2 oz) Parmesan cheese, freshly grated (optional)

Cut the peppers into segments and remove the seeds and tough fibres. Heat the oil and gently cook the garlic and onion. Add the peppers, cover the pan and stew gently for about 1 hour until they practically melt into the oil. Season to taste.

Cook the pasta in 4 litres (7 pints) boiling water with 2 tablespoons coarse salt. Follow the packet directions carefully to avoid over-cooking.

Pass the sauce through a food mill and keep warm.

Drain the pasta, tip into a large, heated serving bowl and stir in the sauce until every strand is coated. Serve at once. If you wish, toss the pasta in grated cheese before adding the pepper sauce, but this is not traditional.

Orecchiette con Cime di Rape

EAR-SHAPED PASTA WITH LEAFY GREEN VEGETABLES

Orecchiette, or 'little ears', is a pasta shape that is unique to Puglia in the 'heel' of Italy. This region was colonized by the Greeks as part of Magna Grecia and in some more remote villages they still speak a dialect of Greek. The older women still wear black and sit outside their whitewashed houses, dextrously sculpting ears of fresh flour-and-water pasta. Around Bari and Monopoli the ears are quite small, but they get larger as you travel down the Salentine peninsula towards Brindisi and Lecce. Some fresh pasta shops outside Italy will make orecchiette to order, and it is possible to buy packets of dried orecchiette. If you cannot find this shape, use shells or penne. In Puglia turnips are grown for their tops and these pungent green leaves are used in this sauce, but broccoli, cauliflower or spring greens can be used instead.

800 g ($1\frac{3}{4}$ lb) trimmed broccoli, cauliflower or spring greens
salt
500 g (1 lb 2 oz) orecchiette, penne or shell pasta
4 tablespoons olive oil
4 cloves garlic, chopped
4 anchovy fillets, chopped
1 small hot chilli pepper, de-seeded and finely chopped

Wash the vegetables and cut into strips or divide into florets. Bring 4 litres (7 pints) of water to the boil, add salt, plunge in the vegetables and cook for a few minutes. Remove the greens with a slotted spoon and then cook the pasta in the same water.

While the pasta is cooking heat the olive oil in a large pan (I use my non-stick wok) and cook the garlic until it begins to colour. Add the anchovy fillets and press them with a wooden spoon so that they 'melt' into the oil. Then add the chilli.

When the pasta is almost cooked, return the vegetables to the pan and cook together with the pasta for 2 minutes. Drain well and stir into the hot oil, garlic and anchovy mixture. Serve at once.

Spaghetti Freddi con Crostacei e Verdure

SHELLFISH SPAGHETTI SALAD

Although I usually prefer traditional pasta recipes I find this new starter from the restaurant 'Il Trigabolo', in Argenta, quite delicious and it has become one of my favourite summer dishes. The original recipe uses the pasta from the Abruzzi region known as spaghetti alla chitarra, so called because the sheets of fresh egg pasta are arranged on a rectangular wooden frame that has tight wires stretching from end to end, like guitar strings. When the rolling pin is pressed over the pasta sheet, the steel wires cut the pasta into thin, flat strips. It is possible to buy dried spaghetti alla chitarra, but the recipe can be made very successfully with ordinary spaghetti, and I think I prefer the texture.

750 g (1½ lb) scampi, prawns (shrimps) or lobster
3 celery stalks
150 g (5 oz) carrots
3 shallots
4 tablespoons extra-virgin olive oil
25 g (1 oz) red sweet pepper (capsicum)
salt and freshly ground black pepper
juice of 1 lemon
500 g (1 lb 2 oz) spaghetti
50 g (2 oz) fresh chives, finely chopped

Clean the shellfish, retaining the heads and shells. Roughly chop half the celery and carrots and 2 shallots and simmer with the heads and shells for 30 minutes.

Process the remaining shallot with the olive oil in a food processor and leave for 30 minutes so that the oil absorbs the flavour.

Chop the remaining celery and carrot and the red pepper into small cubes and lightly steam until tender. Then steam the shellfish until just cooked and reserve the liquid. Divide the shellfish into small segments and season with salt, pepper and lemon juice.

Pour the shellfish stock and the water from the steamer through a strainer and add enough boiling salted water to cook the pasta, following the packet instructions carefully to avoid over-cooking.

Using a small strainer filter the olive oil, discarding the shallot. When the pasta is still very *al dente*, drain and toss with the olive oil and finely chopped chives. Garnish with the shellfish and vegetables.

Bucatini al Sugo di Pesce

PASTA WITH FISH SAUCE

This dish from Campania is usually made with the scorpion fish (rascasse), which gives Mediterranean fish soups their inimitable flavour. When combined with pasta, it makes a wonderfully satisfying one-dish meal.

1 kg (2 lb) scorpion fish (rascasse) or similar strong-flavoured fish, scaled and gutted
3 tablespoons extra-virgin olive oil
1 small onion, finely sliced
2 cloves garlic, peeled
6 fresh basil leaves
3 tablespoons dry white wine
800 g (1¾ lb) canned Italian plum tomatoes, sieved
salt and freshly ground black pepper
500 g (1 lb 2 oz) bucatini, linguine or perciatelli

Rinse the fish and put to drain with the head hanging down.

Heat the oil and gently cook the onion and garlic until very soft. Add the basil, then place the whole fish in the pan, turning it over so that each side cooks gently for about 3 minutes. Add the wine a little at a time. When this has nearly evaporated, pour in the tomatoes and season to taste. Cover and cook gently for about 30 minutes.

Lift the fish from the sauce, removing the head, skin and bones. Discard the garlic and basil. Flake the fish, return to the sauce and keep warm.

Cook the pasta in a large pan of boiling, salted water following the packet directions carefully to avoid over-cooking. Drain the pasta, and stir in the sauce. Serve at once.

Ⓥ Pasticcio di Maccheroni con le Melanzane

BAKED PASTA WITH AUBERGINES

The invading Saracens first introduced aubergines (eggplants) to southern Italy. The Italians believed them to be poisonous, and they were not generally eaten until after the Crusades. When the Sicilian Carmelite monks returned from the Holy Land, they started to serve this now-familiar vegetable to the poor who came to eat at the monastery. When other local people saw that the beggars survived, they began to eat aubergines too.

3 large aubergines (eggplants), thinly sliced
coarse salt and freshly ground black pepper
200 ml (7 fl oz) olive oil
1 onion, chopped
2 cloves garlic, chopped
800 g ($1\frac{3}{4}$ lb) canned Italian plum tomatoes
4 fresh basil leaves
plain (all-purpose) white flour for dredging
500 g (1 lb 2 oz) short pasta such as penne or rigatoni
oil for greasing
300 g (11 oz) Mozzarella cheese, thinly sliced
25 g (1 oz) Parmesan cheese, freshly grated

Sprinkle the aubergines with coarse salt, place in a colander and leave to drain for 30 minutes to 'purge' their bitter juices.

For the tomato sauce heat 1 tablespoon of olive oil and gently fry the onion and garlic until soft. Add the tomatoes with their juice, season, and cook over a high heat so the sauce thickens and retains its bright red colour. Add the basil leaves. Pass the sauce through a food mill or sieve, or blend in a food processor.

Pre-heat the oven to 220°C, 425°F (Gas Mark 7).

Wash the salt off the aubergine slices, dry with a paper towel and flour lightly. Heat the remaining olive oil and fry a few aubergine slices at a time. They should not become too brown or crisp. Remove with a slotted spoon and drain on paper towels.

Cook the pasta in 4 litres (7 pints) of boiling water with 2 tablespoons coarse salt. Cook it briefly until it is pliable but still hard. Drain the pasta and stir into the tomato sauce.

Oil a deep ovenproof serving dish and place a thin layer of pasta at the bottom. Cover with fried aubergines, and then place slices of Mozzarella cheese on top. Add another layer of pasta and repeat the layers, finishing with a layer of Mozzarella that covers the top. Sprinkle on the Parmesan cheese and a little black pepper and bake for 20 minutes or until the top is golden brown.

ⓥ Tarallini con i Finocchietti

LITTLE FENNEL RINGS

In Puglia, where the women always used to work alongside the men in the fields, the traditional pasta sauces had to be quick to prepare, and there are many recipes for bread and biscuits that can be prepared in advance and kept in reserve. These little round, savoury biscuits are sometimes flavoured with chilli pepper, but the most usual taste is fennel seeds.

25 g (1 oz) fresh yeast
1 teaspoon salt
4 tablespoons extra-virgin olive oil
500 g (1 lb 2 oz) plain (all-purpose) white flour
1 tablespoon fennel seeds
oil for greasing

Dissolve the yeast in 3 tablespoons tepid water. Add the salt, the oil and about 250 ml (8 fl oz) tepid water (the exact amount will depend on the quality of the flour). Combine the flour and fennel seeds, then work in the liquid to make a smooth elastic dough. Divide the dough into 24 pieces and roll them out to make finger-sized sausage shapes. Twist each one round to form a ring, using a little water to seal the join. Leave them to rise, uncovered, for about 2 hours.

Pre-heat the oven to 190°C, 375°F (Gas Mark 5).

Bring a large pan of lightly-salted water to the boil. Throw in a few rings at a time, remove them with a slotted spoon the moment they float to the top and drain on paper towels. Oil some baking trays, arrange the rings on them and bake for about 30 minutes.

Ⓥ Minestra di Pasta e Lenticchie

PASTA AND LENTIL BROTH

According to the Old Testament, Esau traded his rights as first-born son for a plate of lentils, and when you savour the great Mediterranean lentil dishes, you can understand why. In Italy there are many tasty pasta and lentil combinations, including this one from Campania, the region around Naples. Use green lentils – they keep their shape when they are cooked – and short pasta, such as tubetti (little tubes), mezze manichi (half-sleeves) or, more poetically, Ave Maria. If you cannot find these shapes, break bucatini or spaghetti into small pieces.

450 g (1 lb) green lentils
3 tablespoons extra-virgin olive oil
3 cloves garlic, chopped
1 small hot chilli pepper, de-seeded and finely chopped (optional)
400 g (14 oz) can Italian plum tomatoes, chopped
2 tablespoons chopped fresh parsley
salt and freshly ground black pepper
300 g (11 oz) tubetti (little tubes)

Wash the lentils under running water, picking out any small stones or twigs, and leave them to soak overnight. Next day rinse the lentils, drain and bring to the boil, without salt, in a large pan of water, then lower the heat. The time they take to cook will depend on the age of the lentils but usually they will take about 20 minutes.

Heat 1 tablespoon olive oil and gently cook the garlic until soft, together with the chilli pepper if used.

When the lentils are cooked, drain them and reserve the cooking liquid. Place the tomatoes in a measuring jug and add lentil cooking liquid to bring the total amount to 1 litre (1¾ pints). Turn into a large pan, add the parsley and garlic mixture, then season to taste. Cook gently for 10 minutes.

Meanwhile, cook the pasta in a pan of boiling, salted water. When it is half-cooked (it should still be hard), drain it and add to the tomatoes. Stir in the lentils and cook gently until the pasta is soft, then serve as a fairly thick broth.

The remaining olive oil is usually dribbled on each serving. Freshly grated Parmesan cheese may also be added but this is not part of the Mediterranean tradition.

(V) Spring Vegetable Paella

When the first young peas and broad (fava) beans are in season, I love to cook this light paella. Many years ago, during my first visit to Spain, our local cook prepared this lovely combination, presenting and serving it from a huge paella. I often make this rice dish and pack it into six tea cups to serve cold. When these are turned out and surrounded by some wild salad leaves they make a very pretty starter.

2 carrots, diced
salt and freshly ground black pepper
3 sweet peppers (capsicums), red, yellow and green
250 g (9 oz) shelled peas
250 g (9 oz) shelled broad (fava) beans
5 tablespoons extra-virgin olive oil
3 cloves garlic, chopped
10 blanched almonds, chopped
$\frac{1}{4}$ teaspoon ground saffron
1 onion, finely sliced
400 g (14 oz) arborio rice, washed and drained
6 artichoke hearts
300 ml (10 fl oz) vegetable stock
10 stoned black olives
3 hard-boiled eggs, sliced

Cook the carrots in boiling salted water. Remove the seeds and tough fibres from the peppers and cut into fine slices. Cook the peas and the broad (fava) beans separately in boiling salted water. When the beans are cooked, drain and remove the skins to reveal the bright green inner bean.

In a flat paella pan heat the oil and gently brown the garlic and almonds. Remove with a slotted spoon and pound to a paste with the saffron.

In the same oil cook the onion and peppers until soft. Stir in the rice and continue to stir until all the grains are coated with oil. Now add the artichokes and carrots, the almond paste and a little hot stock. Simmer until the rice is cooked, adding a little more stock when necessary. Just before the rice is ready gently stir in the beans and peas. Adjust the seasoning if necessary, and garnish with the olives and slices of egg.

Chicken and Rice Pilaff

This is a Lebanese speciality that is very easily made. Traditionally it is made with scrawny free-range chicken, but the dish works well with any available poultry, and there is an interesting range of textures.

4 tablespoons olive oil
1 onion
2 cloves garlic
500 ml (17 fl oz) chicken stock
2.5 cm (1 in) cinnamon stick
400 g (14 oz) boned raw chicken, cut into small pieces
salt and freshly ground black pepper
1 tablespoon lemon juice
300 g (11 oz) risotto rice
4 tablespoons blanched almonds
1 tablespoon pine nuts
2 tablespoons sultanas (white raisins)
1 tablespoon slivered almonds
$\frac{1}{4}$ teaspoon grated nutmeg

Heat 2 tablespoons olive oil and lightly fry the onion and garlic until soft. Heat the chicken stock and put in the cinnamon, onion, garlic, chicken pieces, seasoning and lemon juice. Simmer until the chicken is tender.

Soak the rice in cold water for 30 minutes. Heat the remaining oil and fry the blanched almonds, pine nuts and sultanas. When the nuts are golden brown stir in the drained rice and cook for 5 minutes, stirring continuously. Remove the chicken pieces with a slotted spoon and add to the rice with one-third of the stock. Simmer gently, adding more stock as the liquid is absorbed. If you finish the stock before the rice is cooked, add a little boiling water from time to time. The finished dish should have every grain of rice separate but not dry.

Toast the slivered almonds in a dry pan and sprinkle over the finished dish with the grated nutmeg.

Ⓥ Aubergine Pilaff

In Turkey, pilaff rice is usually served as an accompaniment to the main dish.
When cooking the rice it is important to use the right quantity of water so
that the finished dish is dry and fluffy.

1 medium aubergine (eggplant)
coarse salt and freshly ground black pepper
200 g (7 oz) long-grain rice
6 tablespoons extra-virgin olive oil
2 onions, chopped
2 tablespoons pine nuts
1 large red tomato, peeled and chopped
2 tablespoons currants or sultanas (white raisins)
1 tablespoon sugar
1 teaspoon ground allspice
1 teaspoon ground cinnamon
1 tablespoon chopped fresh dill

Cut the aubergine into 2 cm ($\frac{3}{4}$ in) cubes, sprinkle with coarse salt, place in a colander and leave to drain for 30 minutes. During this time a slightly bitter liquid will drain out; in Italy this is known as 'purging' the aubergine. Soak the rice in hot water with a little salt until the water becomes cold, then drain well.

Rinse and dry the diced aubergine, squeezing out all the water. Heat half the oil and quickly brown the aubergine cubes. Remove them using a slotted spoon, drain on a paper towel and reserve.

Add the rest of the oil to the pan, heat and add the onions, stirring gently. When the onions begin to soften stir in the pine nuts and cook for 10 minutes, then stir in the rice. Fry gently for 15 minutes, stirring with a wooden spoon. Stir in the tomato and cook for 5 minutes. Then return the aubergine to the pan, add all the other ingredients except the dill and pour in 300 ml (10 fl oz) hot water. Bring to the boil, cover, and cook gently until the water is absorbed. Remove from the heat, stir in the dill and season to taste. Place a folded towel over the pan and replace the lid. Leave in a warm place for 15 minutes, then either stir and serve hot or if preferred leave to cool.

Fried Kibbeh Balls

Lina Mahmoud, a Syrian student, showed me how to make these tasty stuffed burghul shells. She was very skilful at hollowing out the space for the filling with her long index finger. I was slower, but I soon found that my food processor went quite a long way towards compensating for unlearned childhood skills.

250 g (9 oz) burghul or cracked wheat
1 onion, roughly chopped
500 g (1 lb 2 oz) lean minced (ground) lamb
salt and freshly ground black pepper

Stuffing
2 tablespoons olive oil
1 medium onion, finely chopped
4 tablespoons pine nuts or chopped walnuts
500 g (1 lb 2 oz) minced (ground) lamb
$\frac{1}{4}$ teaspoon ground allspice
2 tablespoons finely chopped fresh parsley
salt and freshly ground black pepper
olive oil for deep-frying

Begin by making the outer casing. Soak the burghul in warm water for 25 minutes. Put the onion, lamb and seasoning into the food processor and make a smooth paste. Squeeze any excess water out of the burghul, then add to the meat in the processor. Work the mixture until it resembles an elastic pastry dough. Knead well or the shells will crack open while frying.

To make the stuffing, gently fry the onion until soft. Put in the pine nuts and when they are golden brown stir in the meat, spice, parsley and seasoning. Brown the meat, then remove from the heat.

Divide the burghul mixture into 20 small balls. Wet your hands and work each ball in your hands until it is very pliant. Hold the ball in one hand and using your index finger hollow out a hole, rotating your finger to make a large hole and a very thin casing. Spoon in some filling, pinch the hole shut and wet your hands again to smooth out the join. This can be done in advance. When you are ready to serve the kibbeh, deep-fry in hot olive oil at 180°C, 350°F.

ⓥ Panelle

CHICK PEA FRITTERS

The Arab influence is seen all along the Italian coastline, and buckwheat is still called gran saraceno, *while corn is known as* gran turco. *In Liguria chick pea flour (garbanzo or gram flour in Indian cookery) is used to make thin trays of* farinata, *and in Sicily the same flour is used to make these delicious fritters, which are part of the street food* cucina povera *tradition. In Palermo, they are made to perfection by Angelo Maddalena who sells a delectable selection of traditional deep-fried snacks in the Vucciría market. I serve them as pre-dinner nibbles.*

500 g (1 lb 2 oz) chick pea (garbanzo) flour
salt
50 g (2 oz) parsley, chopped
1 teaspoon fennel seeds
olive oil for deep-frying

Put the flour into a heavy saucepan and gradually stir in enough water to make a thick batter, probably about 1.5 litres ($2\frac{1}{2}$ pints). Add a little salt and heat the mixture, stirring all the time as it is cooking. When the mixture has thickened stir in the parsley and fennel seeds.

Lightly oil a large tray and pour out the mixture, using a spoon dipped in cold water to level it out to a depth of 5 mm ($\frac{1}{4}$ in). Allow to cool, then cut into rectangular strips 7 × 10 cm (3 × 4 in). When ready to eat, fry in hot oil at 180°C, 350°F, browning both sides. Serve at once.

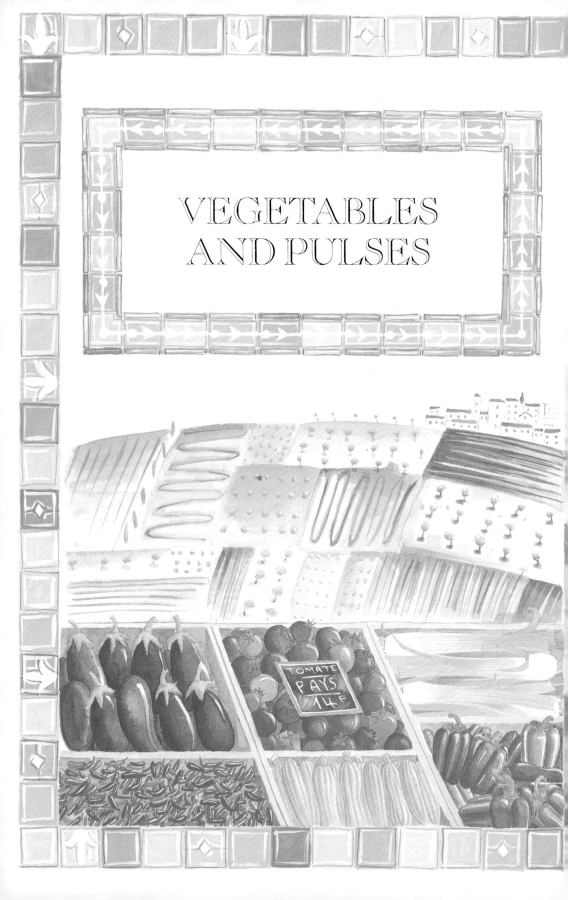

VEGETABLES
AND PULSES

VEGETABLES ARE THE most important part of Mediterranean daily fare. In the past people lived off their kitchen gardens, roaming the hills to add the extra flavour of wild asparagus, pungent green leaves and fresh herbs to their diet. Even in modern Italy I have seen women swiftly putting together delicious bundles of six or seven wild salad leaves, without even moving from the seat they have taken up in the middle of the countryside.

Today the pace of modern life has caught up with Mediterranean countries, and many people live in apartments, without a piece of land to cultivate. Instead they have tomatoes and sweet peppers (capsicums) climbing up balcony railings, and pots of fresh herbs perfume the evening breeze. The street markets have glistening piles of fresh vegetables and everything is enjoyed in its proper season. Artificially-produced vegetables lack the flavour of produce in season, and there is an added pleasure in waiting for the first young peas and beans in the spring, or the mushrooms, pumpkins and artichokes in the autumn.

Many of the vegetables that we associate so firmly with these sunny climes were actually introduced from the New World, and although it is hard to imagine Spanish or Italian cooking without tomatoes and sweet peppers, these were unknown before the sixteenth century. The oldest vegetable is the broad (fava) bean, and aubergines (eggplants) and artichokes, introduced by the Arabs, soon became firm favourites. In hard times people survived on a diet of vegetables and grain, and today we are beginning to appreciate this healthy Mediterranean style of eating.

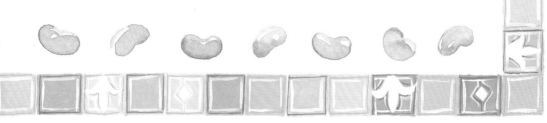

Pizza di Patate

POTATO PIZZA

Puglia, in the 'heel' of Italy, has a tantalizing collection of rustic dishes belonging to the cucina povera *tradition, where great ingenuity was used to make tasty meals from vegetables and a small quantity of more expensive ingredients, such as cheese, ham and eggs. Variations of this recipe are found all over southern Italy, and it is possible to make individual round pizzette in a griddle or heavy pan on top of the stove.*

1 kg (2 lb) floury potatoes, unpeeled
salt and freshly ground black pepper
150 g (5 oz) cooked ham
400 g (14 oz) Mozzarella cheese
50 g (2 oz) butter
1 tablespoon breadcrumbs
3 eggs, beaten
75 g (3 oz) Parmesan cheese, freshly grated
50 g (2 oz) chopped fresh parsley

Pre-heat the oven to 180°C, 350°F (Gas Mark 4).

Put the potatoes into a pan of lightly salted cold water and bring to the boil. Chop the ham and Mozzarella into small cubes. Butter a 23 cm (9 in) shallow pizza pan and dust with breadcrumbs, tapping the pan upside down to shake off the extra crumbs.

When the potatoes are cooked, remove the skin and while still hot purée with a potato masher. Do not use a blender or food processor or the potatoes will acquire a glutinous texture. Stir in the Mozzarella, ham, eggs, Parmesan, parsley, and a little freshly ground black pepper. Mix well, and turn out onto the prepared pan, flattening the mixture with your hands or a rolling pin. It should be about 2 cm ($\frac{3}{4}$ in) thick. Dust with the remaining breadcrumbs, arrange small pieces of butter over the surface and bake in the oven for about 30 minutes.

(V) Polpetes

POTATO CAKES

Clambering over classical sites and going for long, lazy swims work up a prodigious appetite, yet dinner can wait when you sit back and relax with the first drink of the evening, accompanied by little plates of Greek mezethes. These small cheese potato cakes are one of my favourite nibbles, and I often make them at home.

500 g (1 lb 2 oz) potatoes
salt and freshly ground black pepper
100 g (4 oz) Feta cheese, crumbled
4 spring onions (scallions), chopped
3 tablespoons chopped fresh dill
1 egg, beaten
1 tablespoon lemon juice
flour for dredging
3 tablespoons olive oil

Boil the potatoes in their skins with a little salt until soft. (First check how salty the Feta cheese is before you salt the potatoes.) Peel the potatoes while still warm, mash well and stir in the Feta cheese, onions, dill, egg, lemon juice and seasoning. Cover the mixture and leave in the refrigerator to cool.

Divide the mixture into little balls about 2 cm ($\frac{3}{4}$ in) diameter, flatten slightly and dredge them with flour. When ready to serve, heat the oil and fry until they are golden brown on both sides.

ⓥ Insalata in Gelatina

MEDITERRANEAN ASPIC SALAD

Deirdre Galletti has lived in Italy for many years, and although she is English, her whole approach to life has a flavour of the Mediterranean. She is a very creative cook and the food she prepares always has original variations on traditional themes. This elegant salad looks spectacular, yet it can be prepared well in advance. Do not remove from the refrigerator or turn out until ready to serve because, in hot weather, it can start to slip!

250 ml (8 fl oz) de-glazed vegetable stock
15 g ($\frac{1}{2}$ oz) powdered gelatine or a vegetarian alternative
250 ml (8 fl oz) dry white wine
3 cucumbers
salt
5 sweet red tomatoes
$\frac{1}{2}$ yellow sweet pepper (capsicum), de-seeded
1 young carrot
3 tender celery stalks
3 sprigs fresh parsley
10 spring onions (scallions), very finely chopped
6 fresh basil leaves, roughly chopped

Gently heat the vegetable stock, skimming off any fat. Remove it from the heat and sprinkle the gelatine on top. When the gelatine has dissolved, stir in the wine.

Chop half the cucumbers into small cubes, sprinkle with salt and put in a small bowl to expel some of their liquid. Do the same with the tomatoes. Chop the pepper into small cubes. Peel the carrot and, using the serrated end of a corer, if available, cut out small stars. Thinly slice the remaining cucumber and chop the celery into fine crescents.

Put a little gelatine liquid in the bottom of a 1-litre (1$\frac{3}{4}$-pint) ring mould and make an ornamental pattern with the carrot, some of the celery and the parsley. Put in the refrigerator to set. When this has set, dip some slices of cucumber into the remaining gelatine liquid and arrange in an overlapping ring around the mould and up the sides. Return to the refrigerator to set.

Drain the tomatoes and drain and rinse the chopped cucumber. Pat dry so that they do not dilute the gelatine mixture. Chop the spring onions (scallions) very finely and stir together with the tomatoes and basil.

Combine the diced cucumber, pepper and remaining celery crescents.

Arrange a layer of the tomato mixture on top of the cucumber rings and cover with all the celery, cucumber and pepper. Add a layer of the remaining tomatoes and carefully pour in the rest of the gelatine liquid. If there are any cucumber slices left, make another ring around the top.

Cover and refrigerate for at least 3 hours. When ready to serve, dip quickly in boiling water, then turn out onto a large plate. The centre can be filled with cream cheese and chives or drained yoghurt and mint.

(V) Courgette, Pine Nut and Raisin Salad

Many Mediterranean dishes are transformed by the typically Arabic combination of pine nuts and raisins. They are added to meat and fish but show to best effect in simple vegetable dishes. In Sicily they are used to add an unusual touch to spinach, and I am particularly fond of this courgette salad.

500 g (1 lb 2 oz) small courgettes (zucchini)
3 tablespoons olive oil
50 g (2 oz) pine nuts
50 g (2 oz) seedless raisins
1 clove garlic, minced
3 tablespoons finely chopped fresh mint leaves
salt and freshly ground black pepper
2 tablespoons lemon juice

Slice the courgettes into thin discs and fry quickly in the heated olive oil. After a few minutes add the pine nuts and as they begin to change in colour stir in the raisins. Remove the pan from the heat and season with the garlic, mint, salt, pepper and lemon juice. Serve cold.

(V) Aubergines and Chick Peas

*Two of the Mediterranean's favourite ingredients are combined in
this tasty Lebanese stew. Served with crusty bread, it is almost a
meal in itself, but increase the quantities if not serving it with rice
or other dishes.*

200 g (7 oz) chick peas (garbanzos)
3 large aubergines (eggplants)
salt and freshly ground black pepper
4 cloves garlic
4 tablespoons olive oil
2 large onions, chopped
$\frac{1}{2}$ teaspoon ground cumin
$\frac{1}{2}$ teaspoon ground cinnamon
$\frac{1}{2}$ teaspoon ground coriander
1.6 kg ($3\frac{1}{2}$ lb) canned Italian plum tomatoes

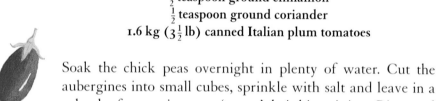

Soak the chick peas overnight in plenty of water. Cut the
aubergines into small cubes, sprinkle with salt and leave in a
colander for 30 minutes to 'purge' their bitter juices. Rinse and
dry with a paper towel.

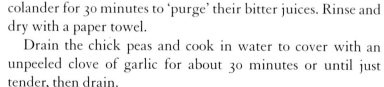

Drain the chick peas and cook in water to cover with an
unpeeled clove of garlic for about 30 minutes or until just
tender, then drain.

Heat the oil and gently cook the onions and remaining
peeled and chopped cloves of garlic until they begin to soften.
Stir in the aubergine cubes. Add the spices and seasoning and
simmer for 5 minutes before adding the tomatoes and cooked
chick peas. Squash the tomatoes with a wooden spoon, cover
and simmer for about 20 minutes, adding a little water if the
mixture becomes too dry. When the aubergines are cooked you
should have a thick stew.

Serve with rice, or use as a side dish with meat or poultry.

Caponata

AUBERGINE APPETIZER

*All Sicilians have their favourite variation on this traditional vegetable dish,
which is usually served cold. It is very versatile as it can be served as antipasto,
a vegetarian main course, or as an accompaniment to meat or fish. Some
people find the sweet-and-sour flavour too unusual for their taste, but I think
it is very good.*

1 kg (2 lb) medium aubergines (eggplants)
salt and freshly ground black pepper
120 ml (4 fl oz) olive oil
2 celery stalks, finely chopped
1 medium onion, finely chopped
400 g (14 oz) canned Italian plum tomatoes, chopped
10 large green olives, stoned
2 tablespoons capers, rinsed and dried
4 anchovy fillets or 3 salted anchovies
5 tablespoons red or white wine vinegar
2 teaspoons sugar
2 tablespoons pine nuts
6 fresh basil leaves

Chop the aubergines into small cubes, sprinkle with salt and leave in a colander for about 1 hour to 'purge' the bitter juice.

Heat half the oil and gently cook the celery for about 15 minutes before adding the onion. When the onion is soft and beginning to change colour remove the vegetables with a slotted spoon and pour in the remaining oil. Turn up the heat, add the aubergines and cook for 10 minutes, stirring continuously. Add the tomatoes, olives and capers. If the capers are very large they should be chopped before they are added to the pan.

Rinse and dry the anchovies and pound to a paste before stirring into the pan. Add the vinegar, sugar and a little pepper, then return the celery and onions to the pan. Simmer for about 15 minutes. When the mixture has thickened, check the seasoning, add the pine nuts and basil and allow to cool.

⒱ Aubergine or Courgette Slices with Garlic and Yoghurt Sauce

Many years ago, when travelling with my daughters in Greece, I discovered this dish in a small taverna in Préveza. It was love at first taste, and we consumed vast platefuls for the rest of the holiday. At home it is equally popular and, if you prefer, it can be made with a combination of vegetables. It is more authentic to deep-fry the vegetables in olive oil but the recipe works with other oils.

6 long aubergines (eggplants) or 6 medium courgettes (zucchini)
coarse salt
300 ml (10 fl oz) natural (plain) yoghurt
3 cloves garlic, minced
olive oil for deep-frying

Slice the aubergines lengthwise into pieces 5 mm ($\frac{1}{4}$ in) thick, cover with coarse salt and leave to 'purge' their bitter juices for at least 45 minutes. Rinse well, then dry the slices. If using courgettes, cut them into similar slices but omit the 'purging' process.

In order to get a thick sauce drain the yoghurt in a muslin-lined strainer for 30 minutes, then stir in a little salt and the minced garlic. You can use more or less garlic according to taste. If you prefer, you can chop the garlic in a food processor with a little yoghurt and then stir it into the rest of the yoghurt.

Heat the oil, deep-fry the vegetable slices in batches until they are golden brown, drain on paper towels and serve immediately with a dollop of yoghurt sauce.

ⓥ Gratin d'Aubergines

AUBERGINE GRATIN

This is a great dish from the south of France, which can be used as a vegetarian main course, or to accompany plain grilled (broiled) meat. If you use it as a main course you will probably need to increase the quantities. Those given here serve six as a side dish.

1.5 kg (3 lb) aubergines (eggplants), stalks removed
5 tablespoons olive oil
3 eggs, separated
150 ml (5 fl oz) milk
3 tablespoons plain (all-purpose) white flour
75 g (3 oz) Parmesan cheese, freshly grated
salt and freshly ground black pepper
4 tablespoons breadcrumbs
25 g (1 oz) butter or 1 extra tablespoon olive oil

Pre-heat the oven to 220°C, 425°F (Gas Mark 7).

Cover the aubergines with lightly salted boiling water, simmer for 5 minutes and then remove with a slotted spoon. When they have cooled enough to handle, chop into small pieces. Heat the oil and gently brown the aubergines.

Beat the egg yolks with a little milk. Stir the flour and grated cheese into the pan with the aubergines, then gradually add the milk. When this is incorporated stir in the yolk mixture. Season to taste and remove from the heat. Whip the egg whites and carefully fold into the mixture.

Turn the mixture into an oiled ovenproof dish and sprinkle over the breadcrumbs. Add a little more black pepper and dot with butter or extra oil. Bake in the oven for about 15 minutes or until it is golden brown. Serve at once.

(V)
Fennel from Provence

Many of my friends do not eat meat, so I often serve this dish with plain grilled fish. However, I love to eat this with roast pork, and I find cooked fennel has an intriguing subtlety.

6 fennel bulbs
4 tablespoons extra-virgin olive oil
salt and freshly ground black pepper
6 tablespoons dry white wine
2 large, ripe, red tomatoes
1 bouquet garni of thyme, bay leaf and parsley

Discard the tough exterior of the fennel, but keep some of the green feathery fonds, if available, for garnishing. Cut each bulb in half and remove the woody core. Cut into very thin slices.

Heat the oil and stir in the fennel, adding salt and pepper to taste. Cover and cook gently for 5 minutes. Pour in the wine, turn up the heat and cook for another few minutes so that some of the wine evaporates. Pour in 200 ml (7 fl oz) water and add the tomatoes and bouquet garni. Cover and stew gently until the fennel is tender and the sauce very thick.

(V)
Tomates à la Provençale

PROVENÇAL TOMATOES

These are very easy to do and they transform a simply grilled (broiled) fish or chop. They are only worth doing with big red tomatoes that have some taste.

6 large red tomatoes
6 tablespoons olive oil
salt and freshly ground black pepper
6 cloves garlic, finely chopped
4 tablespoons finely chopped fresh parsley
50 g (2 oz) fresh breadcrumbs, seasoned

Pre-heat the oven to 220° C, 425°F (Gas Mark 7).

Cut each tomato in half and, using a grapefruit knife, cut out the central seeds. Do not scrape out too much. Heat half the oil and gently cook the tomatoes, cut side down, for 10 minutes. Lightly season the tomatoes and arrange them in an oven dish. Sprinkle the garlic and parsley on top, followed by the breadcrumbs. Drizzle on the remaining oil and put in the oven for 10 minutes. The tomatoes can also be cooked under a hot grill (broiler) for 10 minutes.

ⓥ Kounoupithi

BAKED CAULIFLOWER WITH FETA CHEESE AND TOMATO SAUCE

The cinnamon and lemon juice give this recipe an intriguing flavour and bring a new dimension to the family standby cauliflower cheese. This quantity serves six as a side dish or three as a vegetarian main dish.

4 tablespoons olive oil
3 cloves garlic, finely chopped
1 large onion, finely chopped
800 g ($1\frac{3}{4}$ lb) canned Italian plum tomatoes
1 bay leaf
2 teaspoons dried oregano
2.5 cm (1 in) cinnamon stick
salt and freshly ground black pepper
1 large cauliflower
1 tablespoon lemon juice
150 g (5 oz) Feta cheese

Pre-heat the oven to 190°C, 375°F (Gas Mark 5).

Heat half the olive oil and gently cook the garlic and onion until soft. Add the tomatoes, herbs, spice and seasoning, cover and simmer for 5 minutes. Divide the cauliflower into florets and stir into the sauce. Cover and cook for another 10 minutes. Turn into a shallow ovenproof dish, remove the cinnamon and sprinkle with the remaining olive oil and the lemon juice. Grate the Feta cheese over the top and add a little more black pepper. Bake in the oven for 25 minutes.

(V) Couscous aux Sept Legumes

COUSCOUS WITH SEVEN VEGETABLES AND SPICES

Every country has a mystical lucky number that gives rise to recipes with a specific number of ingredients. In India it is the number nine, and Navrattan recipes, while in Morocco it is seven, as in this couscous from Fez.

100 g (4 oz) chick peas (garbanzos)

Stock: 1 celery stalk, 2 onions, 4 cloves garlic, 1 small hot chilli pepper, salt, 4 cm ($1\frac{1}{2}$ in) cinnamon stick

3 aubergines (eggplants)
salt
750 g ($1\frac{1}{2}$ lb) couscous
4 small turnips, peeled and quartered
7 carrots, chopped
7 courgettes (zucchini), sliced
500 g (1 lb 2 oz) pumpkin, sliced
4 large red tomatoes, sliced
4 tablespoons chopped fresh coriander leaves
4 tablespoons chopped fresh parsley
5 tablespoons olive oil
$\frac{1}{2}$ teaspoon turmeric
$\frac{1}{4}$ teaspoon ground allspice
$\frac{1}{4}$ teaspoon ground ginger
$\frac{1}{4}$ teaspoon ground saffron
$\frac{1}{2}$ teaspoon paprika
$\frac{1}{4}$ teaspoon ground cinnamon
$\frac{1}{2}$ teaspoon ground black pepper
harissa paste (optional)

Soak the chick peas in plenty of cold water overnight. Next day, drain and put on one side.

Roughly chop the stock vegetables, cover with 1 litre ($1\frac{3}{4}$ pints) water, add the cinnamon and some salt and bring to the boil. Simmer for an hour, then strain, discarding all the vegetables.

Cut the aubergines into thirds, sprinkle with salt and leave in a colander for at least 30 minutes to 'purge' their bitter juice, then rinse and dry.

Put the couscous in a shallow bowl and cover with tepid water. Drain at once and set on one side so that the couscous starts to swell.

Bring the stock to the boil and put in the chick peas, turnips and carrots. Rub the couscous to separate the grains and transfer to a muslin-lined steamer or couscousier. Steam on top of the chick peas and vegetables, running a fork through the grains every so often to keep them separate and fluffy. After 25 minutes remove the grain and transfer to a flat plate. Sprinkle on a little hot, lightly salted water and cover with a cloth.

Add the sliced courgettes, pumpkin, tomatoes, aubergines, coriander and parsley to the pan and simmer gently for 10 minutes. Heat the oil and work half of it into the grain. In the remaining oil lightly sweat the spices, then stir them into the vegetables.

Arrange a border of couscous around the outside of a large serving platter and heap the vegetables in the middle with a little of the cooking juice. The rest of the juice can be served separately with a little harissa added. A small bowl of harissa can be put on the table so that each person can decide how 'hot' to make their couscous.

(V) Mücver

COURGETTE FRITTERS

Last summer I spent some time on board a gulet *– a Turkish coasting vessel – off the Mediterranean coast, and the great stores of fresh vegetables which were loaded on board at every stop appeared in a new guise at each mealtime. We were most enthusiastic about the mücver which Askin, the cook produced in his very hot little galley. This is his recipe.*

1 kg (2 lb) courgettes (zucchini), grated
2 onions grated
3 eggs, beaten
150 g (5 oz) Feta cheese, crumbled
2 tablespoons plain (all-purpose) white flour
1 tablespoon chopped fresh dill
salt and freshly ground black pepper
4 tablespoons olive oil

Put the courgettes and onions in a colander for 30 minutes to drain. Turn into a bowl and stir in the eggs, cheese, flour, dill and seasoning.

Heat the olive oil and fry a tablespoon of the mixture at a time. Brown both sides, then remove with a slotted spoon and place on a paper towel to drain. Keep warm while cooking the rest of the fritters. Serve hot.

(V) Fagioli Stufati al Pomodoro

BEANS IN TOMATO SAUCE

*This has little in common with the perennial nursery favourite.
Years ago on one of my first visits to Puglia I was not terribly
thrilled when I heard what was on the menu for supper. It seemed
to me a long way to travel for sausage and beans. The sausages,
however, home-made and quite delicious, were grilled (broiled) on
the great open fire, and the cindery terracotta bowl revealed that
the beans had stewed slowly overnight in the same fireplace,
nestling in the warm embers. It was a feast, and the beans are
almost as good when cooked with more modern equipment. I often
cook the beans in a terracotta casserole in a slow oven, but they
can be cooked on top of the stove too.*

500 g (1 lb 2 oz) cannellini or borlotti beans
4 tablespoons extra-virgin olive oil
1 large onion, finely chopped
2 cloves garlic, finely chopped
2 celery stalks, finely chopped
2 carrots, finely chopped
800 g (1¾ lb) canned Italian plum tomatoes, sieved
salt and freshly ground black pepper
1 tablespoon chopped fresh parsley

Soak the beans overnight in plenty of cold water. Drain them,
cover with cold water and bring to the boil. Simmer slowly for
about 1½ hours or until tender, then drain, reserving the cooking
liquid. This time will vary, depending on the age and quality
of the beans. Heat the oil and gently fry the onion, garlic, celery
and carrots. When the onion begins to change colour, stir in
the tomatoes and season to taste. When the pan begins to boil,
stir in the beans, cover and stew gently for at least an hour,
adding a little bean water from time to time if the sauce becomes
too thick, but every bean should be coated. Just before serving
stir in the chopped parsley.

ⓥ Dried Broad Bean Purée

To the uninitiated this might sound dull but it is as delicious as the better-known chick pea (garbanzo) purée hummus. Since ancient times the broad (fava) bean has been one of the great sources of nourishment around the Mediterranean. Every country has a traditional recipe in which this humble bean is transformed by an anointing of very good olive oil. I have sampled versions in Greece, Turkey, Italy, Egypt, Tunisia and Morocco and they are all delicious. Here is byesar *from Morocco.*

200 g (7 oz) skinned dried broad (fava) beans
4 garlic cloves, peeled
$\frac{1}{2}$ teaspoon ground cumin
4 tablespoons extra-virgin olive oil
salt
$\frac{1}{4}$ teaspoon dried oregano
cayenne or black pepper

Soak the beans overnight in plenty of cold water. Rinse, drain, bring to the boil in water to cover, and simmer gently with the whole garlic cloves and cumin for $1\frac{1}{2}$ hours or until soft. Drain, reserving a little cooking water, and purée in a food processor. Add 3 tablespoons olive oil and salt to taste. If the mixture seems too dry add a little of the reserved cooking liquid but do not 'drown' the beans.

Serve cold in a bowl sprinkled with a little oregano and cayenne or black pepper, and dribble the remaining olive oil over the purée.

(V) Eggs with Sweet Peppers and Tomatoes

The Turkish name for this dish is menemen. *Most recipes for it suggest beating the eggs before stirring them into the cooked vegetables. This produces a dish very similar to the Basque* piperade. *When I was in Turunç, in southern Turkey, one of the small, simple eating places served a very interesting* menemen *with whole eggs broken into scooped-out hollows in the vegetable mixture. I found this version more interesting, and if I am cooking for several people I use two medium pans but for two people I usually use small individual pans.*

2 tablespoons olive oil
3 onions, chopped
3 red or yellow sweet peppers (capsicums)
4 large, ripe tomatoes, chopped
1 tablespoon chopped fresh parsley
salt
6 eggs
cayenne pepper (optional)

Heat the oil in a 18–20 cm (7–8 in) pan and fry the onions until soft. Remove the seeds and tough membranes from the peppers, chop, add to the onions and fry gently until cooked. Add the tomatoes and cook for 5 minutes. Stir in the parsley and add salt to taste. Make six little hollows in the mixture and gently break in the eggs. Cover and cook until the whites are set but the yolks still runny. If you like 'hot' food sprinkle on a pinch of cayenne pepper. Serve at once.

Ⓥ Revuelto de Esparragos

SCRAMBLED EGGS AND ASPARAGUS

These creamy scrambled eggs can be made with young green asparagus but in Spain they are usually made with the thin green asparagus that grows wild on the hillsides in the Mediterranean spring. It is sometimes possible to find little bundles of it for sale by the side of the country roads in southern Spain, and the women use them in many local specialities. They are much more bitter than cultivated asparagus and so they have to be cooked for much longer.

500 g (1 lb 2 oz) young green asparagus
salt and freshly ground black pepper
50 g (2 oz) butter
10 eggs
6 tablespoons milk

Scrape the stringy threads from the asparagus and break off the tough, inedible bottom of the stalks. Cook in boiling, salted water until tender. Drain, cut into 4 cm ($1\frac{1}{2}$ in) lengths, then toss in the melted butter in a heavy pan. Beat together the eggs and milk, season to taste and stir into the pan with the asparagus. Stir with a wooden spoon until the eggs begin to set, but remove the pan from the heat while they are still very creamy. Serve as a starter with some good crusty bread. Increase the quantities if you want to serve it as a main course.

Ⓥ Saganaki

FRIED CHEESE

The name of this appetizer comes from the small two-handled pan in which the cheese is fried. It appeals to all ages, as we discovered on a family holiday on the Greek island of Spetse, when this cheese dish was inevitably demolished before it could reach the person who had ordered it at the other end of the table!

6 slices Kasseri or other hard cheese, each about 4 × 7.5 cm ($1\frac{1}{2}$ × 3 in)
in size and 5 mm ($\frac{1}{4}$ in) thick
flour for dredging
olive oil
freshly ground black pepper
green olives

Lightly dust the cheese slices with flour. Cover the base of a frying pan with a thin coating of oil and when it is sufficiently hot fry the cheese until golden brown on both sides. Serve at once with some black pepper and a few green olives to the side.

ⓥ Tortilla Española

SPANISH OMELETTE

This is a perennial favourite found all over Spain. To make a tortilla that is about 2.5 cm (1 in) thick use a 15 cm (6 in) frying pan.

3 large floury potatoes
3 tablespoons olive oil
2 large Spanish onions, finely sliced
salt and freshly ground black pepper
6 eggs, beaten

Peel the potatoes and cut them into small cubes. Heat the oil and fry the potatoes for a few minutes before adding the onions and seasoning. Cover and cook gently until the vegetables are soft, stirring from time to time. Remove the vegetables with a slotted spoon and stir them into the eggs. Return the mixture to the pan, cover and cook over a low heat. When the eggs begin to set around the edges gently lift up the rim with a knife to allow the liquid to run to the bottom of the pan. When the top is still slightly runny, cover the pan with a plate and carefully tip the tortilla upside down on to the plate. Then slide it back into the pan to cook the other side. This dish can be served hot as a light lunch or supper but I also love it cold, cut into small wedges for picnics or tapas-like nibbles.

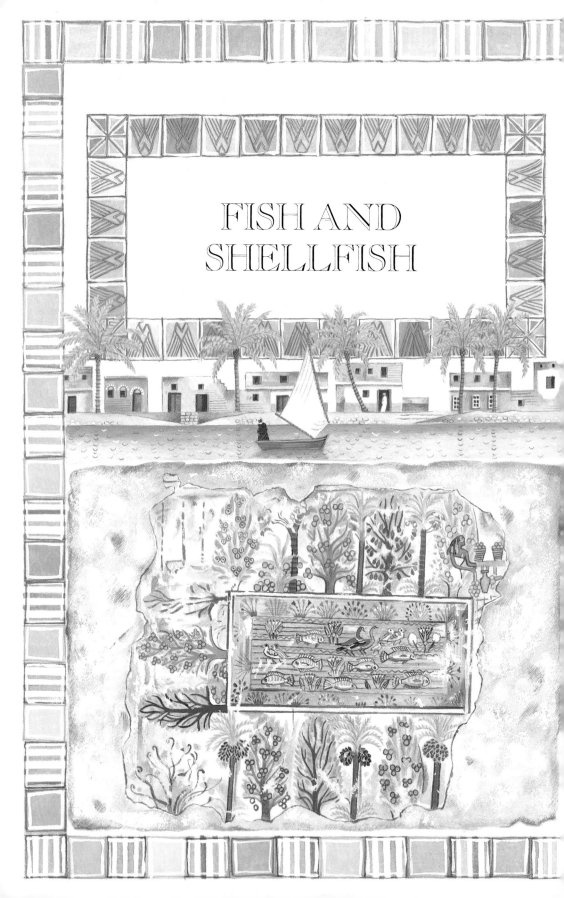

FISH AND SHELLFISH

THE WARM, SHALLOW
waters of this land-locked sea are not an ideal habitat for
fish, yet Mediterranean seafood continues to be one of
the great gastronomic pleasures in life. In the time of the
Caesars, in the splendid villas along the Italian coast, fish
were lured into a labyrinth of stone channels, constructed
to ensure that the Roman patricians could have a constant
supply of fresh fish.

In the Mediterranean, fish is usually served very simply
and freshness is considered all important. Traditionally
in restaurants the uncooked fish is carefully chosen by the
customer, who inspects eyes, gills and firmness of flesh
before deciding on a particular fish. In these days when
the price of fish has soared it is a good idea to get the raw
fish weighed in front of you, to avoid any shock when the
bill comes.

In the past the Church imposed 'lean' periods of the
year when meat, eggs and dairy produce could not be
eaten, and 'Clean Monday', the first day of Lent in Greece,
is still an occasion when meat dishes are banished and
fish reigns supreme. Since Mediterranean fish is so good
there seems little self-denial in this custom, and now that
the Church has relaxed its 'fast' days the demand for fish
has, if anything, increased, and it cannot be satisfied by
catch from the local waters. Today fish is flown in from
all corners of the world, and the fish displayed in the local
markets has often started its life in a very different sea.

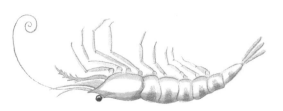
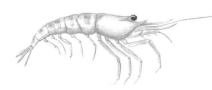

Gambas Pil Pil

HOT PRAWNS

In Spain this little starter is served in small, flat, terracotta dishes, and if your dishes are flameproof it can be cooked on top of the stove. I prepare it in advance, then pop it in a hot oven for about 5 minutes just before we are ready to eat. It makes a deliciously easy-to-prepare appetizer. If uncooked 'green' prawns (shrimps) are unavailable this recipe can be made with cooked prawns.

500 g (1 lb 2 oz) small prawns (shrimps), unshelled
3 cloves garlic, chopped
1 hot chilli pepper, crushed
salt
3 tablespoons olive oil

Shell the prawns, remove the central back vein, and pat dry. Divide the prawns between 6 small oven dishes and add the garlic, chilli pepper, salt and olive oil. Leave to marinate for at least 2 hours, but longer if it is more convenient.

Cook either over a high heat or in a pre-heated oven at 240°C, 475°F (Gas Mark 9), for 5 or 10 minutes, then serve sizzling hot.

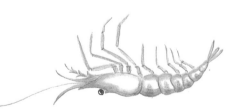

Gambas con Gabardina

PRAWNS IN OVERCOATS

These prawns (shrimps) are fried in a light, crisp, beer batter and served as a tasty nibble to accompany a glass of dry sherry in the Spanish 'tapas' tradition. I love this batter and I often make a double quantity, dip in courgette (zucchini) batons and artichoke segments and serve a heap of these cooked vegetables beside the prawns as a wicked starter. Cooked prawns may be used if uncooked 'green' prawns are unavailable.

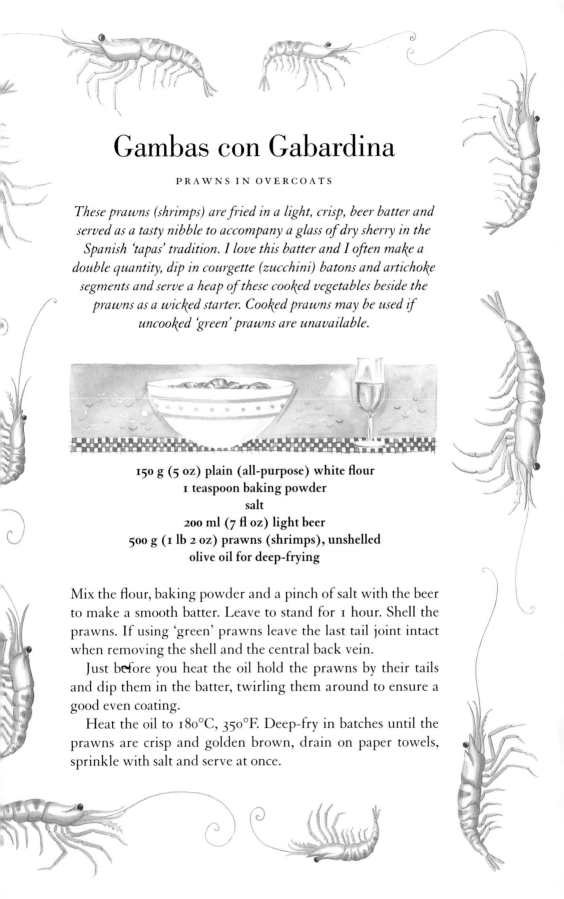

150 g (5 oz) plain (all-purpose) white flour
1 teaspoon baking powder
salt
200 ml (7 fl oz) light beer
500 g (1 lb 2 oz) prawns (shrimps), unshelled
olive oil for deep-frying

Mix the flour, baking powder and a pinch of salt with the beer to make a smooth batter. Leave to stand for 1 hour. Shell the prawns. If using 'green' prawns leave the last tail joint intact when removing the shell and the central back vein.

Just before you heat the oil hold the prawns by their tails and dip them in the batter, twirling them around to ensure a good even coating.

Heat the oil to 180°C, 350°F. Deep-fry in batches until the prawns are crisp and golden brown, drain on paper towels, sprinkle with salt and serve at once.

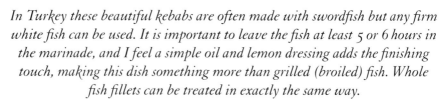

Fish Kebabs

In Turkey these beautiful kebabs are often made with swordfish but any firm white fish can be used. It is important to leave the fish at least 5 or 6 hours in the marinade, and I feel a simple oil and lemon dressing adds the finishing touch, making this dish something more than grilled (broiled) fish. Whole fish fillets can be treated in exactly the same way.

750 g ($1\frac{1}{2}$ lb) swordfish or firm-fleshed white fish fillets, 2 cm ($\frac{3}{4}$ in) thick
salt

Marinade
1 medium onion
120 ml (4 fl oz) olive oil
120 ml (4 fl oz) lemon juice
salt
8 bay leaves

Lemon dressing
120 ml (4 fl oz) extra-virgin olive oil
120 ml (4 fl oz) lemon juice
4 tablespoons chopped fresh parsley
salt and freshly ground black pepper

Wash and dry the fish, salt lightly and leave for 10 minutes in a large flat glass or china dish. If you intend to thread the fish on skewers cut it into 4 cm ($1\frac{1}{2}$ in) cubes. If you prefer whole fillets, cut into single-portion pieces.

Pulp the onion in a food processor and mix with the olive oil, lemon juice and a little salt to make the marinade. Pour over the fish. Cover with the bay leaves and leave for 5 to 6 hours. At the end of this time arrange on skewers (or leave in single portions), and grill (broil) under a pre-heated hot grill for about 8 minutes on each side, basting frequently with the marinade liquid.

Combine all the lemon dressing ingredients together and pour over the fish when it has been arranged on individual plates.

Daurade Baked in Paper

This is a classic way of cooking fish, and I particularly enjoy this Turkish version where the fish is marinated and cooked in a combination of olive oil, lemon and onion juice.

1 medium onion
3 cloves garlic, finely chopped
100 g (4 oz) fresh parsley, finely chopped
200 ml (7 fl oz) extra-virgin olive oil
150 ml (5 fl oz) lemon juice
salt and freshly ground black pepper
3 daurade (gilt-headed bream) or similar white fish
each fish to serve 2 portions, gutted and scaled

Pre-heat the oven to 190°C, 375°F (Gas Mark 5).

Reduce the onion to thick liquid in a food processor, then mix with the garlic, parsley, olive oil, lemon juice and seasoning to make the marinade. Make 3 deep slashes horizontally on both sides of each fish. Rub the marinade into the cuts and leave the fish to marinate for at least 2 hours in a glass or china dish, turning over half-way through.

When ready to cook, place each fish in the middle of a generous rectangle of baking parchment, pour over a little marinade and fold carefully to make a parcel. Pinch the edges tightly to make a good seal. I usually put in a few staples on the long side. Sprinkle a little water on the top of each of the parcels and bake in the oven for about 30 minutes. If you are using smaller fish to give each person their own parcel, reduce the cooking time to 20 to 25 minutes. I always bring the packets to the table so that everyone enjoys the aroma as the parcels are slashed, and I get help with dividing up the fish!

Fried Mussels with Walnut Sauce

This walnut sauce is served in Greece and Turkey with fried or grilled (broiled) chicken, fish, aubergines (eggplants) and courgettes (zucchini). In Kuşadasi I escaped from the romantic, seventeenth-century caravanserai *hotel, with its beautiful courtyard but disappointing, bland, tourist food, to discover the local cooking. I sat near a small jetty with a bottle of chilled white wine, watching the little fishing boats making their evening preparations, enjoying the selection of* mezes. *The electricity came and went throughout the evening and we were often eating in sudden darkness. During a black-out I took an enchanting mouthful of what turned out to be a crisp, deep-fried mussel, dipped in this delicious walnut sauce.*

Walnut sauce
2 thick slices stale white bread
4 large cloves garlic
150 g (5 oz) shelled walnuts
200 ml (7 fl oz) extra-virgin olive oil
120 ml (4 fl oz) lemon juice
salt and freshly ground black pepper

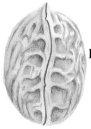
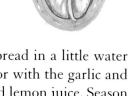

1 kg (2 lb) large mussels
salt and freshly ground black pepper
juice of 1 lemon
plain (all-purpose) white flour for coating
2 eggs, beaten
100 g (4 oz) breadcrumbs
olive oil for deep-frying

Make the sauce. Remove the crusts and soak the bread in a little water until soft. Squeeze dry and place in a food processor with the garlic and walnuts. Grind coarsely, then slowly add the oil and lemon juice. Season to taste. If you find the sauce too thick you can add a little water.

Scrape the mussels under running water, removing the 'beard' and discarding any open or broken shells. Cook in boiling, lightly salted water until the shells open. Discard any mussels that remain closed, and remove the others from their shells. Season the mussels, squeeze on a little lemon juice, then roll in flour, beaten egg and breadcrumbs. Deep-fry a few at a time until they are golden brown. Remove with a slotted spoon and drain on paper towels. Keep them warm while you cook the remainder.

Serve the hot mussels arranged on a large serving dish with the bowl of walnut sauce. You can eat the mussels with toothpicks if they are not very large.

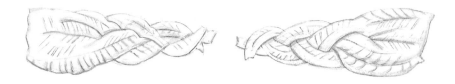

Sole Fillets in Citrus Fruit Sauce

I have found variations of this recipe in Spain, France and Italy, and it works well with any delicate white fish. I often use small Mediterranean sole fillets which can be quickly plaited to give a very pleasing presentation.

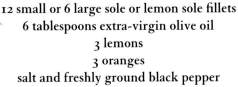

12 small or 6 large sole or lemon sole fillets
6 tablespoons extra-virgin olive oil
3 lemons
3 oranges
salt and freshly ground black pepper

Pre-heat the oven to 180°C, 350°F (Gas Mark 4).

If you are using small fillets and you want to make a plait, use kitchen scissors to cut each fillet into 3 strands, leaving them joined at one end. Make a neat plait, season to taste and place 2 at a time on small pieces of kitchen foil, brushed with olive oil. If you are using whole fillets, place these in pairs on foil, brushed with olive oil. Fold the edges of the foil packets very tightly to make a good seal, and cook in the oven for 15 minutes.

With a zester remove some fine threads of peel from 1 lemon and 1 orange, and reserve for decoration. Then peel all the oranges and lemons, removing all the white pith. Divide into segments, discarding skin and pips (seeds). I usually do this over a wide bowl to catch the juice. Cut the fruit into small cubes and heat gently with the juice and olive oil. Add a little salt and black pepper. Do not stew the fruit or allow the mixture to come to the boil.

Remove the fish from the foil and arrange on individual dinner plates, with a little sauce spooned over the top. Decorate with a few fine threads of zest. Serve hot.

Corfu Fish Stew

I have never eaten this fish stew when visiting Corfu, but a Greek friend, from Rhodes, often cooks her version of 'Corfu' fish stew. It is easy to make, works well with most fish, and has a rich, garlicky flavour.

4 tablespoons extra-virgin olive oil
1 large onion, finely sliced
2 carrots, cut into rounds
2 celery stalks, chopped
1 kg (2 lb) potatoes, peeled and finely sliced
6 cloves garlic, chopped
salt and freshly ground black pepper
1 kg (2 lb) fish fillets
juice of 2 lemons

Heat 3 tablespoons of oil and gently cook the onion until soft. Add the carrots, celery and potatoes. Stir with a wooden spoon for a few minutes until the vegetables are coated with oil, then add the garlic and allow the mixture to begin to change colour before adding enough water to cover the contents of the pan. Add seasoning, then cover and cook gently for 15 minutes.

Cut the fish into small pieces and add to the pot, stirring gently with a wooden spoon to avoid breaking up the fish. Add a little more water if necessary but be careful not to 'drown' the fish. Most of the liquid should be absorbed by the time the fish and vegetables are cooked. After 10 minutes pour in the lemon juice and check the seasoning. Remove the pan from heat and let it stand for 5 minutes. Pour on the remaining olive oil and serve at once.

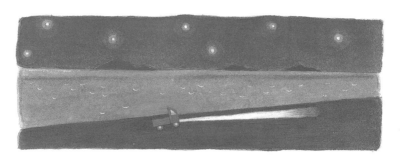

Lobster with Lemon Sauce

*Many years ago, when staying on the Greek island of Kéa, we used to eat
every night at the same small taverna. The taverna was several kilometres
from our hotel, so in the early evening the owner, Kosta, would pick us up by
boat on his way back from setting his overnight fishing nets. When we had
finished our meal, and after he had consumed many, many ouzos, he would
return us to the hotel in his spluttering three-wheeler, lurching precipitously
over potholes in the narrow, curving dust track that was the coast road. Only
our greed and the 'international' menu at the hotel gave us the courage to
face this nightly Russian roulette of a drive. When the sea had yielded a
disappointing catch Kosta would say, sadly and apologetically, 'I am afraid it
will have to be lobster again tonight.' We always accepted this 'blow' with
equanimity, and discovered how much we loved his simple way of cooking
his 'second-best' offering.*

**200 ml (7 fl oz) white wine vinegar
salt and freshly ground black pepper
3 small rock lobsters
150 ml (5 fl oz) extra-virgin olive oil
juice of 2 lemons
6 medium potatoes (optional)
2 tablespoons chopped fresh oregano or parsley**

Heat a large pan of water and when it comes to the boil add the vinegar,
a little salt and the lobsters. Bring back to the boil, then lower the heat
and cook for about 8 minutes. Remove the lobsters, cut each in half
lengthwise and take out the vein. Only the tail meat is used and this
should be loosened from its shell and cut into small slices.

Whisk together the oil and lemon juice and season to taste. This sauce
can be poured over the lobster or served separately.

Kosta's wife used to boil a few potatoes with the lobster and serve
potato slices, moistened with a little of the cooking liquid, as a bed for the
lobster tails, and then pour over the lemon dressing and sprinkle with
oregano or parsley.

Merluza con Salsa Verde

HAKE WITH GREEN SAUCE

This fish casserole is a universal Spanish favourite, and I learned to make it many years ago from a Spanish friend, Luisa Clifton. We often used cod instead of hake and found it very good, even without clams and mussels to decorate the finished dish. It can also be cooked in individual oven dishes.

6 tablespoons extra-virgin olive oil
6 hake or cod steaks, 2 cm ($\frac{3}{4}$ in) thick
2 tablespoons plain (all-purpose) white flour,
plus extra for dredging
salt and freshly ground black pepper
2 tablespoons lemon juice
6 tablespoons chopped fresh parsley
12 mussels (optional)
12 clams (optional)
1 large onion, chopped
6 cloves garlic, chopped
200 ml (7 fl oz) dry white wine
200 ml (7 fl oz) fish stock
300 g (11 oz) shelled peas

Pre-heat the oven to 180°C, 350°F (Gas Mark 4).

Heat the oil and gently fry the lightly floured and seasoned fish until golden brown on both sides. Remove with a slotted spoon and arrange in a large flat casserole or 6 small dishes. Sprinkle with lemon juice and a little of the parsley.

If using shellfish bring them to the boil in a little salted water, and cook quickly until the shells open. Discard any that fail to open. Pour the cooking liquid through a strainer and reserve.

Gently fry the onion and garlic until soft in the same pan used for the fish, then stir in 2 tablespoons flour and a little of the reserved shellfish water (or plain water) to make a smooth paste. Gradually stir in the wine and enough fish stock to make a thick sauce. Then add the peas and parsley. Stir well, check the seasoning and pour over the fish steaks. Cook for 15 minutes in the oven, arranging the reserved shellfish on top for the last 3 minutes.

Trote alla Vernaccia

TROUT COOKED IN VERNACCIA WINE

Sardinia was under Spanish domination for many years, and the local wine, vernaccia, bears a strong resemblance to sherry, even though the vine grown in Oristano is unlike the Jerez Palomino. Local legend has it that Saint Giustina caused the first vines to flourish, watering them with copious tears as she commiserated with the poor, malaria-ridden populace. Chilled vernaccia is a good aperitivo, *and it is used to enhance many local dishes. If you cannot find vernaccia this recipe can be made with dry sherry.*

4 tablespoons extra-virgin olive oil
1 carrot, finely chopped
2 cloves garlic, finely chopped
4 tablespoons finely chopped fresh parsley
1 sprig fresh rosemary, finely chopped
1 teaspoon finely chopped fresh oregano
6 trout, gutted and cleaned
salt and freshly ground black pepper
350 ml (12 fl oz) vernaccia or dry sherry

For this recipe, you will need 2 large frying pans, each taking 3 fish. Heat the oil and gently cook the carrot, garlic and herbs until quite soft. Arrange the fish on top, season and pour on the wine. Cover and cook gently for 20 minutes. Remove the fish and serve with the sauce and small boiled potatoes.

Triglie al Forno con Olive

RED MULLET WITH OLIVES

Lecce in Puglia reached its greatest glory under the Spanish, and the city is full of baroque yellow limestone buildings dating from that era. The older hotels with their decaying grandeur have a melancholy charm, but the dining rooms are still a triumph, serving finely prepared, traditional regional dishes made from top-quality local produce. Only cook this recipe if you have very fresh fish.

6 mullet, gutted and cleaned
250 g (9 oz) stoned black olives
salt and freshly ground black pepper
3 tablespoons good-quality white wine vinegar
4 tablespoons extra-virgin olive oil

Pre-heat the oven to 180°C, 350°F (Gas Mark 4).

Arrange the fish in a single layer in a large, flat oven dish. Surround the fish with the olives, season with salt and pepper, then pour over the vinegar and oil. Bake the fish in the oven for about 20 minutes. In Italy the dish is turned round after 10 to 15 minutes to ensure that the fish cooks evenly.

Andalucian Fried Fish

Andalucia is famous for its fried food and one of the great pleasures in life is to sit at a simple eating place near Seville's old Triana market, with a glass of fino, eating crisp, greaseless, fried fish. Although it is quite extravagant to fry in olive oil, the results are well worth it, and it is quite safe to filter the oil and use it again. For deep-frying, I use one of the less expensive, mass-produced, pure olive oils.

6 fillets or cutlets of hake, cod or whiting
coarse salt
plain (all-purpose) white flour for dredging
olive oil, 3 cm ($1\frac{1}{4}$ in) deep, for frying
6 lemon segments

Sprinkle the fish with salt and leave for at least 30 minutes. Brush off excess salt and dredge with flour. Heat the olive oil to 180°C, 350°F, and fry the floured fish until golden brown. Remove with a fish slice, drain on paper towels and serve *at once* with lemon wedges.

Capesante alla Adriatica

SCALLOPS ADRIATIC STYLE

Along the Adriatic coast small, tasty scallops are cooked very simply so that their flavour is not masked by other ingredients.

3 tablespoons extra-virgin olive oil
2 cloves garlic, finely chopped
3 tablespoons chopped fresh parsley
18 scallops
salt and freshly ground black pepper
juice of 1 lemon
2 tablespoons breadcrumbs

Pre-heat the oven to 180°C, 350°F (Gas Mark 4). Wash and dry 6 scallop shells.

Heat the oil and gently fry the garlic. When it begins to turn colour remove from the heat and stir in the parsley. If the scallops are large cut in half, if not leave whole and allow 3 per serving. Arrange on the shells, season and spoon on a little garlic mixture, lemon juice and a sprinkling of breadcrumbs. Put them in the hot oven until they are golden brown. Remove and serve immediately.

Calamari Ripieni

STUFFED SQUID

Variations of this dish can be found near the sea in every region of Italy. I like to serve it as an unusual starter.

3 small ripe tomatoes, peeled
150 g (5 oz) shelled prawns (shrimps)
6 tablespoons dry white wine
salt and freshly ground black pepper
juice of 2 lemons
4 tablespoons extra-virgin olive oil
3 cloves garlic, minced
1 teaspoon hot minced chilli pepper (optional)
50 g (2 oz) fresh breadcrumbs
2 tablespoons chopped fresh parsley
12 small squid, prepared

Pre-heat the oven to 180°C, 350°F (Gas Mark 4).

Cut the tomatoes into quarters, remove the seeds, then chop and put to drain in a colander. Boil the prawns (shrimps) for a few minutes in the white wine, remove with a slotted spoon and season with salt, pepper and a little lemon juice. Divide the prawns into small pieces.

Heat 3 tablespoons oil and gently fry the garlic and chilli until the garlic begins to change colour. Remove from the heat and stir in the breadcrumbs, parsley, tomatoes and prawns. Stuff each squid sac with this mixture, season to taste, add a squeeze of lemon and a few drops of the remaining oil and wrap in a small square of foil.

Bake for 20 minutes in the oven. Serve hot in the foil packets so that all the aromas are preserved.

Aurióu au Four

BAKED MACKEREL

The herb fennel works magic with most fish, and this simple recipe from Provence is quite delicious.

6 medium, whole mackerel, gutted and cleaned
salt and freshly ground black pepper
1 bunch fennel
6 large ripe tomatoes, thickly sliced
100 g (4 oz) fresh breadcrumbs
3 tablespoons extra-virgin olive oil

Pre-heat the oven to 180°C, 350°F (Gas Mark 4).

Wash and dry the fish, then rub the insides with salt and pepper. Arrange half the fennel over the bottom of a flat oven dish and cover with tomato slices. Line up the fish on top and garnish with the remaining fennel. Scatter the breadcrumbs over this and pour on the olive oil. Bake in the oven for 30 minutes, spooning a little cooking juice over the top from time to time.

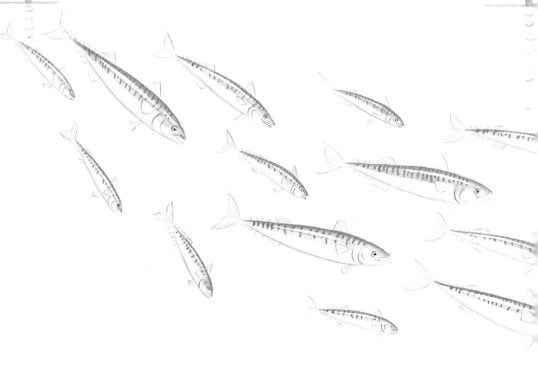

Maquereaux Grillés au Cumin

GRILLED MACKEREL WITH CUMIN

In Djerba, the land of the lotus eaters, mackerel is cooked very simply on the grill (broiled) after it has been marinated for 30 minutes in olive oil and spices. Mackerel has never been my favourite fish but when I tried it cooked this way, straight from the sea, I understood why Ulysses' sailors desired to stay put, even without the lotus!

1.5 kg (3 lb) medium, whole mackerel
5 tablespoons olive oil
3 teaspoons ground cumin
4 cloves garlic
salt
1 teaspoon harissa paste or cayenne pepper
2 lemons

Clean the fish and remove the heads. Mix together the oil, cumin, minced garlic, salt and harissa paste diluted in 6 tablespoons water. Make 2 deep diagonal cuts in each side of the fish, and put the fish in the marinade, pushing the marinade into the slashes with a wooden spoon.

Cook the fish over charcoal or under a pre-heated grill (broiler) for about 8 minutes each side. Cut the lemons into wedges and serve one with each sizzling hot fish.

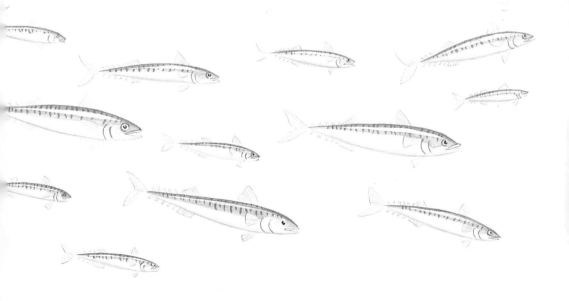

Estoco-fi à la Niçoise

SALT COD NICE FASHION

The Mediterranean was introduced to salt cod by the Norwegians and it soon became an important part of the gastronomic heritage in the Iberian peninsula, southern France and Italy. By the early nineteenth century the demand was so great that the Norwegians established a stoccafisso *warehouse in Venice. When Venice was besieged by the Austrians in 1849 this warehouse fed the entire population, including the cats!*

1 kg (2 lb) salt cod
4 tablespoons extra-virgin olive oil
2 onions, finely chopped
1 leek, finely chopped
1 red sweet pepper (capsicum), de-seeded and thinly sliced
1.2 kg (2½ lb) canned Italian plum tomatoes
2 cloves garlic, peeled and crushed
1 bouquet garni of thyme, bay leaf, parsley and fennel
freshly ground black pepper
750 g (1½ lb) potatoes, peeled and sliced
100 g (4 oz) black olives

Soak the salt cod for 3 days, changing the water every day. If possible leave it some of the time under running water. When ready to cook, drain the fish, pat dry and remove skin, bones and any discoloured flesh. Cut into pieces about 5 cm (2 in) long.

Heat the oil and gently cook the onions, leek and sweet pepper until soft. Do not allow to change colour. Put in the tomatoes with their juice and the crushed garlic, bouquet garni and fish. Add a little freshly ground black pepper and simmer for an hour. Now put in the potatoes and olives and cook for another 20 minutes. Remove the bouquet garni and serve.

Esqueixada

SALT COD SALAD

I had never been tempted to try this dish until I saw it prepared by Rosa Grau of Barcelona's 'Florian' restaurant. I found it quite delicious and it makes an easy, unusual starter.

300 g (11 oz) salt cod
1 small onion, very finely sliced
3 tablespoons extra-virgin olive oil
1 tablespoon sherry vinegar
freshly ground black pepper
3 ripe large red tomatoes
2 green sweet peppers (capsicums), de-seeded
12 black olives

Soak the salt cod in cold water for 3 days, changing the water daily. If possible leave it some of the time under running water. Remove any skin, bones, discoloured flesh and tough threads. Dry the fish very well to remove any water, then tear to shreds with your fingers.

Add the finely-sliced onion to the shredded fish. Mix together the oil and vinegar and pour over the fish and onion. Grind a little back pepper over and leave to cure for 3 hours.

Plunge the tomatoes briefly into boiling water, peel, discard the seeds and grate the flesh. Cut the peppers into matchsticks and blanch in boiling water. Allow to cool.

When ready to serve, stir the tomatoes and peppers into the fish and garnish with black olives.

POULTRY

POULTRY HAS ALWAYS
played an important rôle in Mediterranean cooking, and
every country, regardless of race or creed, has a great
collection of sumptuous dishes, where fruit, vegetables,
herbs, nuts or yoghurt are combined with chicken to
produce a great meal. Mediterranean chickens tend to
look rather scrawny when compared with some other
plump birds, but these *polli ruspante*, scratching out a
living, stalking round backyards, road sides and open
ground, have far more flavour than the confined variety,
and over the years recipes have been developed to
counteract their defects. Even today, when many
Mediterranean chickens are artificially fed, they still taste
special when prepared with fresh herbs and spices.

In some regions wild duck are shot to give more variety
to the table, and Ernest Hemingway used to follow up a
day's duck shooting in the Venetian lagoon with a plate
of pasta and duck sauce, as served in the 'Trattoria alla
Maddalena' on the island of Mazzorbo.

Most of the recipes in this section can be prepared using
any available poultry, and the exotic is not always the
more tasty. The Romans ate geese, ducks, turkeys, doves
and peacocks but the poet Horace, who had a large farm
between Tivoli and Subiaco, declared that there was little
difference between the taste of peacock and chicken! So
who needs a peacock?

Chicken with Walnut and Coriander Sauce

This dish was given to me by a Greek family from Rhodes. I have never found it in Greece, and I think it would probably feel more at home in Turkey.

120 ml (4 fl oz) extra-virgin olive oil
6 chicken pieces
250 ml (8 fl oz) dry white wine
400 ml (14 fl oz) chicken stock
4 bay leaves
salt and freshly ground black pepper
2 large cloves garlic
150 g (5 oz) shelled walnuts
2 tablespoons whole coriander seeds
$\frac{1}{4}$ teaspoon cayenne pepper
juice of 3 lemons
3 eggs

Heat 2 tablespoons olive oil in a flameproof casserole and lightly brown the chicken pieces on both sides. Stir in the wine and bring to the boil, scraping the pan to incorporate any browned bits. Add the stock, bay leaves and salt and pepper. Cook slowly on top of the stove until the chicken is tender (about 30 minutes).

In a food processor blend together the garlic, walnuts, coriander and cayenne pepper. Slowly, as if you were making mayonnaise, add the remaining olive oil and half the lemon juice. Mix well and season to taste.

With a slotted spoon, remove the chicken pieces from the casserole and keep warm. Pour the casserole juices through a strainer and stir them into the walnut sauce.

In a separate bowl, beat the eggs until light and frothy, then stir in the remaining lemon juice. Transfer the egg mixture to a saucepan and slowly stir in the walnut sauce. Heat gently but do not allow the sauce to boil. Pour the sauce over the chicken pieces and serve straight away.

Cerkez Tavugu

CIRCASSIAN CHICKEN

In the harems of another era the Circassian women were prized for their great beauty, and this north-easterly region of Turkey is still famous for its lovely inhabitants. In a more prosaic age, and perhaps with a touch of sour grapes, beauty is often equated with a lack of brains, and the adjective 'Circassian' is often used to suggest stupidity. However, when it is used gastronomically, it still evokes admiration, because it means the sumptuous chicken and walnut appetizer that continues to grace the meze table. *This is the version served by Mrs Tarakçi at her 'Hotel Diplomat' in Turunç.*

1.5 kg (3 lb) chicken
2 onions, peeled and quartered
1 carrot
salt
3 slices stale white bread
2 cloves garlic
400 g (14 oz) shelled walnuts
1 tablespoon walnut or extra-virgin olive oil
$\frac{1}{2}$ teaspoon paprika or cayenne pepper

Gently cook the chicken in a covered pan with the onions, carrot, salt and enough water to cover. Allow to cool in its own stock.

Remove the crusts and soak the bread in a little of the chicken stock. Process the squeezed-out bread, garlic and walnuts with a little stock to make a smooth paste. Transfer to a pan and gradually, over a low heat, stir in enough of the chicken stock to make a thick pouring sauce. Keep one-third of the sauce to one side. Allow the sauce to cool.

Pull the chicken off the bone and divide into small pieces. Stir the chicken pieces into the larger portion of walnut sauce, making sure every piece is well coated. Arrange them on a large flat serving plate, and pour the remaining sauce on top to mask the chicken. It is traditional to dribble on some walnut oil obtained by squeezing crushed walnuts in a cloth. I have never managed to obtain any oil this way, so I usually dribble on a little commercially-prepared walnut or extra-virgin olive oil and a dusting of paprika or cayenne pepper.

Chicken with Quince

This recipe illustrates how good Greek home cooking can be. Quinces are used in a myriad of ways all round the Mediterranean, but although I love the tawny jelly and preserves, I think the recipes combining quince with poultry and meat are my real favourites. Out of season it is possible to substitute pears.

2 quinces
1 tablespoon lemon juice
1 kg (2 lb) chicken, cut into 6 pieces
plain (all-purpose) white flour for dredging
salt and freshly ground black pepper
3 tablespoons olive oil
1 large onion, chopped
2 cloves garlic, chopped
400 g (14 oz) canned Italian plum tomatoes
2.5 cm (1 in) cinnamon stick
2 tablespoons chopped fresh mint

Peel and core the quinces, cut into quarters and slice thickly. Cover with cold water and lemon juice to prevent them turning brown. Lightly dredge the chicken pieces with seasoned flour. Heat half the oil and brown the chicken on all sides. Drain the quince slices and dry with a paper towel. Remove the chicken pieces and lightly brown the quince slices, lift out with a slotted spoon and put to one side. Add the rest of the olive oil and gently cook the onion and garlic until soft but not brown. Return the chicken pieces to the pan and stir in the tomatoes, squashing them against the side of the pan with a wooden spoon. Add the cinnamon stick, a little water and seasoning. Cover and simmer gently for 20 minutes, then return the quince slices to the pan. Cook for another 15 to 20 minutes, then stir in the chopped mint and cook for another 5 minutes. Before serving remove the cinnamon stick.

The dish is equally good if cooked in advance and the fresh mint added just before re-heating.

Middle Eastern Yellow Chicken

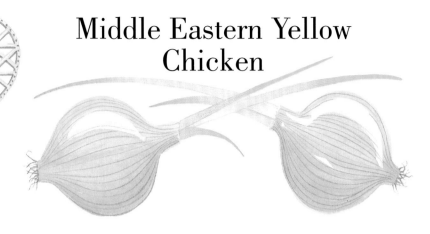

In Tunisia, chicken joints are marinated and then cooked on skewers over large charcoal grills. This works well at barbecues, but at home I usually marinate the chicken quarters, wrap them in foil and cook them in a moderate oven for 20 minutes. I then open the top of the foil packets and let the chicken brown for another 10 minutes.

2 large onions, peeled
150 ml (5 fl oz) lemon juice
salt
6 chicken quarters
$\frac{1}{2}$ teaspoon ground saffron
2 tablespoons olive oil

In a food processor reduce the onions to pulp and mix with the lemon juice and a little salt. Arrange the chicken in a shallow glass or china dish and pour over the marinade. Leave for at least 5 hours or more if this suits you better. Turn the chicken over from time to time so that the marinade permeates every part.

Pre-heat the oven to 190°C, 375°F (Gas Mark 5). Cut 6 pieces of kitchen foil and arrange a piece of chicken in the centre of each with a spoonful of the marinade. Fold over the foil to seal and place on a baking tray with the seam upwards. Cook in the oven for 20 minutes. Dissolve the saffron in the oil. Open the packets and brush the top of each chicken piece with the saffron oil. Cook for another 10 minutes or until golden brown.

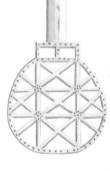

Chicken and Avocado Salad

*An unusual starter from Israel using citrus fruits and avocado
pears. I was served my starter in the intact skin of half an avocado,
but this is a little tricky for six people with only two avocados, so I
like to use my white avocado-shaped dishes. If you are using avocado
skins to serve in, sprinkle on a little lemon juice to stop them going
black too quickly.*

500 g (1 lb 2 oz) chicken breast or 1 small chicken
salt and freshly ground black pepper
1 small onion, chopped
1 celery stalk, chopped
1 green sweet pepper (capsicum), de-seeded
1 orange
2 tablespoons chopped blanched almonds
4 tablespoons mayonnaise
2 avocado pears
2 tablespoons lemon juice
2 lettuce leaves

Cook the chicken in simmering, salted water with the onion
and celery. Discard the liquid and allow the chicken to cool,
then dice it into small pieces. Cut the pepper into matchsticks.
Peel the orange, making sure you remove all the white pith
and inner skin. Cut into thin slices. Mix together all these
ingredients with seasoning, the almonds and mayonnaise, and
keep in a cool place.

Just before serving cut the avocados in half and remove the
skin and stone (seed). Cut into small cubes and sprinkle with
lemon juice. Slice the lettuce into ribbons. Stir the avocado and
lettuce into the chicken mixture and serve at once.

Chicken Casserole with Orange and Avocado

This dish was prepared for me many years ago by one of my Israeli students living in Rome. I adopted it as a favourite summer dish, served with pilaff rice.

6 chicken breast fillets
salt and freshly ground black pepper
3 tablespoons extra-virgin olive oil
2 tablespoons cornflour
$\frac{1}{2}$ teaspoon ground allspice
400 ml (14 fl oz) orange juice
2.5 cm (1 in) cinnamon stick
3 oranges, peeled
2 avocado pears

Season the chicken and fry gently in the oil until golden brown on both sides. Mix the cornflour and allspice to a smooth paste with a little orange juice, then stir into the remaining juice. Pour over the chicken, add the cinnamon and stir until the sauce thickens. Cover and cook gently for about 25 minutes, or until the chicken is tender.

Divide the oranges into segments, removing the pips (seeds), pith and white inner skin. Cut into smallish pieces, reserving the juice that runs out while you do this. Peel the avocados and cut each half into thin slices. Sprinkle on the reserved orange juice and cut each slice into 3. Add to the chicken and simmer for a few minutes to heat the fruit. Serve at once.

The first part of this recipe can be prepared in advance, then re-heated just before the prepared fruit is added.

Chicken Cooked in Yoghurt

It is often impossible to decide whether a particular recipe is of Greek or Turkish origin. I have eaten this in the small Turkish town of Kas, near Antalya, and I have not come across many Greek dishes cooked in yoghurt, but a dear Greek friend claims this is a traditional Greek dish.

2 tablespoons olive oil
1 large onion, chopped
2 cloves garlic, chopped
2 tablespoons plain (all-purpose) white flour
200 g (7 oz) Greek yoghurt
$\frac{1}{2}$ teaspoon ground cumin
1 tablespoon chopped fresh mint
salt and freshly ground black pepper
2 eggs, beaten
3 chicken breasts
50 g (2 oz) hard cheese (e.g. Parmesan or Cheddar), grated

Pre-heat the oven to 180°C, 350°F (Gas Mark 4).

Heat the oil and gently cook the onion and garlic until soft but not brown. Beat the flour into the yoghurt, then add the cumin, mint and seasoning. Stir in the eggs. Divide each chicken breast into 6 small pieces and season. Arrange in a single layer in a large, shallow, terracotta casserole with the onions and garlic. Pour over the yoghurt mixture and sprinkle with cheese and black pepper. Bake in the oven for about 40 minutes or until the chicken is tender, and the yoghurt is solid and golden brown. Serve hot.

Chicken à la Niçoise

Around the flower market in 'old' Nice it is still possible to find little eating places serving traditional dishes, and this combination of moist chicken, glistening black olives and crisp slices of courgettes (zucchini) and aubergines (eggplants) is a perennial favourite.

3 courgettes (zucchini)
3 aubergines (eggplants)
6 tablespoons extra-virgin olive oil
1 large or 2 small chickens, jointed
3 onions, finely chopped
1 red sweet pepper (capsicum), de-seeded and sliced into rings
400 g (14 oz) canned Italian plum tomatoes
$\frac{1}{2}$ teaspoon ground saffron
salt and freshly ground black pepper
50 g (2 oz) small black olives
4 cloves garlic, finely chopped
6 fresh basil leaves, finely chopped

Cut each courgette and aubergine into 4 lengthwise and cover with a little coarse salt. Place in a colander to drain. Heat 2 tablespoons of oil and gently fry the chicken pieces until they are golden brown on both sides. Remove with a slotted spoon and set aside.

Add 2 tablespoons of oil to the pan in which you fried the chicken and gently cook the onions and red pepper. When these are soft pour in the tomatoes and turn up the heat so that some of the juice evaporates. Return the chicken to the pan with the saffron dissolved in a teaspoon of warm water. Season to taste, cover and cook gently for about 30 minutes.

Rinse the vegetables in the colander and dry well. Just before serving the chicken, fry the vegetables in the remaining oil until golden brown.

Arrange the chicken on a large, shallow serving dish, sur-rounded by the fried vegetables and black olives. Sprinkle the garlic and basil on top.

Chicken Dafina

Orthodox Jews cannot cook after sundown on Friday until the end of the Sabbath, and traditionally a complex, rich casserole was carried in advance to the baker's shop to cook slowly overnight in the hot embers of the bread oven, ready for Saturday lunch. This dafina *is a North African version of a* cholent. *A flour and water paste is used to seal the lid on the casserole.*

250 g (9 oz) chick peas (garbanzos)
12 small chicken pieces
3 onions, finely chopped
4 cloves garlic, peeled
800 g ($1\frac{3}{4}$ lb) canned Italian plum tomatoes
12 pitted dates
1 teaspoon salt
$\frac{1}{4}$ teaspoon black pepper
$\frac{1}{2}$ teaspoon ground cinnamon
$\frac{1}{4}$ teaspoon ground ginger
$\frac{1}{4}$ teaspoon turmeric
$\frac{1}{2}$ teaspoon ground allspice
200 g (7 oz) long-grain rice, washed and drained
12 small potatoes, scrubbed but not peeled
6 unshelled, uncooked eggs
100 g (4 oz) plain (all-purpose) white flour

Soak the chick peas (garbanzos) in plenty of cold water for at least 12 hours.

Pre-heat the oven to 120°C, 250°F (Gas Mark $\frac{1}{2}$).

Take a large casserole that will hold all the ingredients and spread the drained chick peas over the bottom. Arrange the chicken pieces on top, covered and surrounded by the onions, garlic, tomatoes, dates, seasoning and spices.

The rice should be placed on a double layer of muslin which is then tied at the top to form a bag. Leave enough room for the rice to swell as it cooks. Place this bag on top of the chicken in the middle of the dish, and arrange the potatoes and whole eggs alternately round the bag. Pour in enough water to nearly cover the ingredients, leaving at least 2.5 cm (1 in) space between the water level and the lid.

Mix enough water with the flour to make an elastic dough and knead until smooth. Roll out the dough to make a thin sausage the length of the rim of the casserole. Press this between the lid and the casserole very firmly to make a good seal. Bake in the oven for at least 12 hours.

To serve, run a pointed knife round the pastry seal and remove the lid. Traditionally the *dafina* was eaten in stages, and the shelled eggs are usually served in advance with the potatoes and some of the broth.

Syrian Chicken

Many Mediterranean countries have recipes where the great coarse loaves are hollowed out and filled with tasty meat and gravy. In this variation round, flat, crusty bread is used to line a deep casserole. Sumac is a deep red powder made from dried berries and it can usually be found in Middle Eastern stores. It has a sour taste and sometimes I substitute Indian kokum or tamarind. Failing this, try lemon juice.

**2 or 3 large round, flat loaves
3 large onions, finely sliced
salt and freshly ground black pepper
50 g (2 oz) ground sumac
12 small chicken pieces
3 tablespoons extra-virgin olive oil**

Pre-heat the oven to 220°C, 425° (Gas Mark 7).

Slice the loaves in half so that there are two large flat discs. Cut these into regular pieces and use them to line a deep round oven dish with the soft side inwards. Save enough pieces to form a lid. Arrange in the dish a layer of half the onions and season well with salt, pepper and a third of the sumac.

Put the chicken pieces on top of the onions and season with salt, pepper and half the remaining sumac. Dribble half the oil over the chicken, then cover with the rest of the onions and sumac. Season well with salt and pepper. Place pieces of bread to cover all the casserole with the crusty side outwards, and pour over the remaining oil.

Bake in the oven for about 50 minutes. If the top begins to get too brown, cover with a sheet of foil.

Fesenjan

DUCK IN WALNUT AND POMEGRANATE SAUCE

The courtly Persian cooking influenced not only the Indian cuisine but also that of Turkey and the rest of the Middle East. Merchants brought new tastes to Venice, which was for many years the gateway to the East and the centre of the spice trade. This recipe reminds me of the Venetian speciality, roast turkey with pomegranate sauce.

400 g (14 oz) shelled walnuts
4 tablespoons olive oil
2 onions, very finely sliced
$\frac{1}{2}$ teaspoon turmeric
salt and freshly ground black pepper
2 × 1.5 kg (3 lb) ducklings, jointed into 4
5 pomegranates
2 tablespoons sugar
4 tablespoons lemon juice

Chop the walnuts until they resemble coarse breadcrumbs. Heat half the oil and gently cook the onions and turmeric until the onions are soft. Remove the onions with a slotted spoon and put into a pan with the walnuts, seasoning and about 1 litre ($1\frac{3}{4}$ pints) of water. Stir well, bring to the boil and let the sauce reduce. Arrange a wooden spoon across the pan, place the lid on top, and cook gently for 20 minutes.

Remove all visible fat from the joints of duck and cook in the onion-pan oil, adding more oil as necessary. Brown all the pieces on both sides, then add to the pan containing the walnut mixture. Spoon the mixture over the duck so that all the joints are covered. Put on the lid, ensuring that it fits very tightly, and cook slowly until the duck is very tender.

Cut the pomegranates in half and scoop out the flesh and seeds. Put in a food processor to break up the seeds, then strain the juice. Mix with the sugar and lemon juice.

When the duck is cooked skim off as much fat as possible before adding the fruit pulp. Cook for another 15 minutes, check the seasoning and, if necessary, add more lemon juice or sugar to get the sweet-sour balance that pleases you.

Chicken Kofta

There are many Middle Eastern recipes for little balls of minced chicken. I like to serve them for nibbles before dinner parties. Although it is possible to use cooked chicken, they are much more successful if you make them with raw white meat.

1 slice stale white bread
300 g (11 oz) chicken breast, skinned and boned
1 tablespoon chopped fresh parsley
juice of 1 lemon
salt and freshly ground black pepper
50 g (2 oz) shelled, peeled pistachio nuts
2 tablespoons sesame seeds
plain (all-purpose) white flour
olive oil for deep-frying

Remove the crusts and soak the bread in a little warm water. Squeeze dry. Put the chicken into the food processor and reduce to a smooth paste. Add the parsley, lemon juice, bread and seasoning. Now add the pistachio nuts and process briefly so that little crumbs of pistachio remain apparent. Put the mixture in the refrigerator for at least 30 minutes.

Divide the mixture into small balls the size of a large marble. Roll in the sesame seeds and return to the refrigerator until ready to cook. Lightly dust with flour and fry in hot oil until golden brown.

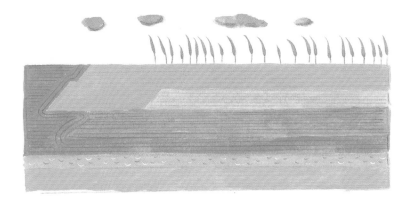

MEAT

ROUND THE
Mediterranean there are no lush pasture lands, and the
animals are usually slaughtered young to save on fodder.
Most of the traditional cheeses are made with goat's or
ewe's milk, and butter and cream are fairly 'new'
ingredients. The favourite meat is young lamb and goat,
grilled (broiled) on the spit, flavoured with aromatic
herbs or spices, and traditionally this was the great dish
to be enjoyed on 'high' days and holidays. The other meat
was often tough and stringy, so long slow casseroles were
created to make it more appetizing and digestible. Meat
was not eaten every day, and often vegetables, pulses and
grain products were combined with the more expensive
meat to make it go further.

Until about fifty years ago most rural families in the
north-western Mediterranean kept a pig, which when
slaughtered provided a variety of cuts that could be
preserved to eke out the family's meagre daily winter
fare. This explains the great variety of dry salami-type
sausages and hams found in the gastronomic heritage of
Spain and Italy. The Muslims and Jews were forbidden
to eat this by their religion so in North Africa and the
Middle East there are no traditional pork recipes. The
Roman Catholic and Greek Orthodox Churches used to
have strict rules about 'lean' days when meat could not be
eaten, and Lent was the period of the most drastic dietary
restrictions. The great annual feasting that climaxed in
mardi gras or 'fat Tuesday' became known as *Carnivale*,
from the Latin *carne vale*, or 'farewell meat', which was
banished from the table once Ash Wednesday arrived.

Lamb Souvlakia Marinated in Yoghurt

In countries where the meat tends to be a little tough it is often marinated in yoghurt to help it become more tender. Even top-quality meat gains from this treatment. In Greece and Turkey, onion juice is used to give extra flavour, and the cooks seem adept at wringing juice from reluctant onions. I always end up with hands that reek of onion for days, and a feeling of deep frustration as I inspect my meagre results. I now substitute very finely chopped onion.

1 medium onion, finely chopped
200 g (7 oz) Greek yoghurt
3 cloves garlic, minced
salt and freshly ground black pepper
1 kg (2 lb) lean lamb, cut into 5 cm (2 in) cubes
7–8 bay leaves
2 tablespoons olive oil

Stir the onion into the yoghurt with the garlic and seasoning. Cover the lamb with this mixture and lay the bay leaves on top. Leave to marinate overnight or for 10 to 12 hours, stirring the mixture a couple of times.

When ready to cook the meat, lightly oil 6 long kebab skewers and thread on the cubes of meat, shaking off the excess yoghurt. Do not pack the cubes of meat too closely together or they will not cook evenly. If you do not have long skewers, it is better to use more than 1 skewer per person. Brush the kebabs with olive oil and add a little more salt and pepper before cooking under a hot grill (broiler). Turn the kebabs over while cooking to make sure they are evenly cooked. The meat should be crisp on the outside but soft and tender inside. You must decide how pink the meat is to remain.

Lamb Casserole

In Greece there are various recipes in which the food is baked in a sealed container so that no delicious aromas can escape. Some stories tell that during the Greek War of Independence women used to cook food in a clay water jug and carry it up the mountains to their guerrilla husbands. This ensured that the men's position was not given away by tell-tale cooking fires. Another story describes how meat and vegetables were wrapped in sealed packets, so that the smell of cooking would not attract hungry brigands roaming the countryside for plunder. In this recipe a flour and water paste is used to seal the lid on a terracotta casserole, in the manner of a Provençal daube.

100 g (4 oz) flour
1 kg (2 lb) lean boned lamb, cut into 5 cm (2 in) cubes
6 medium potatoes, finely sliced
3 onions, finely sliced
3 large cloves garlic, finely chopped
1 celery stalk, chopped
6 small sprigs fresh rosemary
1 tablespoon dried oregano
1 teaspoon dried thyme
1 tablespoon chopped fresh dill
2 tablespoons lemon juice
3 tablespoons extra-virgin olive oil
salt and freshly ground black pepper

Pre-heat the oven to 120°C, 250°F (Gas Mark $\frac{1}{2}$).

Mix enough water with the flour to make an elastic dough and knead until smooth. Cover and set aside.

In a casserole that will just hold all the ingredients place the lamb and the potatoes, onions and garlic. Add the celery, herbs, lemon juice, olive oil, seasoning and 1 tablespoon of water. Roll out the dough to make a thick sausage the length of the rim of the casserole. Press this between the lid and the casserole very firmly to make a good seal. Bake in the oven for at least 2 hours. Leave to cool for 10 minutes before inserting the point of a sharp knife to cut through the pastry seal. Serve hot.

Roast Lamb with Quince Stuffing

Although similar recipes can be found in Spain and North Africa, this recipe comes from the Greek islands and it is one of my favourite autumn dishes. If you cannot buy fresh quinces, substitute pears or quince preserve.

2 kg (4½ lb) boned leg of lamb
2 tablespoons olive oil
juice of 2 lemons
1 tablespoon dried oregano
salt and freshly ground black pepper

Stuffing
4 tablespoons extra-virgin olive oil
1 medium onion, chopped
50 g (2 oz) long-grain rice, washed and drained
2 quinces, peeled and chopped
50 g (2 oz) blanched almonds, chopped
1 teaspoon ground cumin
200 ml (7 fl oz) light stock
2 tablespoons chopped fresh parsley
juice of 2 lemons
salt and freshly ground black pepper

Make the stuffing. Heat the oil and gently fry the onion until soft. Stir in the rice and the quinces and coat well with the oil. Add the almonds and cumin. Pour in the stock, stir well, cover and cook gently for about 20 minutes until the stock has been absorbed and the rice is cooked. Stir in the parsley and lemon juice and season to taste. Leave the stuffing to cool completely.

Pre-heat the oven to 220°C, 425°F (Gas Mark 7).

Fill the cavity where the bone was in the meat with stuffing and sew up the opening. Rub the meat with oil, lemon juice, oregano and seasoning. Place in the oven for 10 minutes, then turn down the heat to 190°C, 375°F (Gas Mark 5), and cook for an hour.

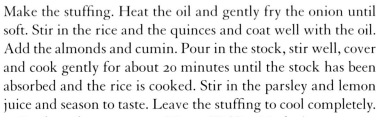

Gigot d'Agneau à la Provençale

ROAST LEG OF LAMB PROVENÇAL STYLE

Although the lamb is best cooked on a spit with the vegetables roasting underneath in a pan of succulent meat juices, the same sort of effect can be gained by roasting the meat on the grids of an oven shelf, with the vegetables roasting underneath on a lower shelf.

2.5 kg (5½ lb) leg of lamb
2 cloves garlic
salt and freshly ground black pepper
2 teaspoons dried thyme
6 potatoes, peeled and thinly sliced
2 tablespoons olive oil
6 large red tomatoes
3 onions, thinly sliced
6 small sprigs fresh rosemary

Pre-heat the oven to 230°C, 450°F (Gas Mark 8).

Keep the meat at room temperature for at least 1 hour before roasting. With a pointed knife make a series of deep incisions in the meat and place in thin slivers of garlic. Rub salt, pepper and thyme over the meat and place on a shelf or rack in the oven. Put a large roasting tin containing 50 ml (2 fl oz) water on the shelf below to catch the juices.

Arrange the potatoes in a shallow ovenproof dish which contains 2 tablespoons olive oil with alternate slices of tomato and onion. Tuck a few tiny sprigs of rosemary among the potatoes. Gently moisten with 50 ml (2 fl oz) water and season to taste. I am usually quite generous with the freshly ground black pepper.

When the meat has been in the oven for 15 minutes reduce the temperature to 190°C, 375°F (Gas Mark 5). Pour any juices which have collected in the roasting pan over the vegetables, and put the vegetable dish inside the roasting pan below the meat. The vegetable dish will get a little dirty on the outside but this cannot be avoided. Roast the meat until cooked to your taste. Allow about 20 minutes per 450 g (1 lb). The vegetables need to have a little water added from time to time. Remove the meat from the oven, carve and serve with the vegetables.

Garlic Veal or Beef Stew

In Corfu this rich beef stew is called sofrito, *and I find this name a culinary mystery. It would seem to come from the island's Italian past, since, in Italian,* soffritto *is the gentle frying of onions and garlic in olive oil, which is the first stage in many recipes. Yet the classic version of this dish contains no onions, and only the meat has this preliminary frying. But whatever the origin of its name, it is an unusual, pungent, marvellously satisfying casserole. It needs the sort of slow cooking that used to be done in the village baker's oven once the daily bread was baked. A flour and water paste is used to seal the lid on the casserole.*

150 g (5 oz) plain (all-purpose) white flour
1 kg (2 lb) lean veal or beef, trimmed and cut into 2.5 cm (1 in) cubes
salt and freshly ground black pepper
3 tablespoons olive oil
150 ml (5 fl oz) red wine vinegar
6 bay leaves
1 tablespoon dried rosemary
1 tablespoon dried thyme
15 cloves garlic, peeled

Pre-heat the oven to 120°C, 250°F (Gas Mark $\frac{1}{2}$).

Mix 100 g (4 oz) of the flour with enough water to make an elastic dough and knead until smooth. Cover and set aside. Roll the cubed meat in the remaining flour, seasoned liberally with salt and pepper. Heat the olive oil and brown the meat on all sides. With a slotted spoon remove the meat to a casserole and then stir the vinegar into the frying pan, scraping off and incorporating any brown crusts adhering to the pan. Simmer for a few minutes, then pour over the meat in the casserole. Add the bay leaves, herbs, the whole garlic cloves and about 150 to 200 ml (5 to 7 fl oz) water. Roll out the dough to make a sausage the length of the rim of the casserole. Press this between the lid and the casserole very firmly to make a good seal. Cook in the oven for about 3 hours.

When you remove the casserole from the oven, leave it to stand for 10 minutes before breaking the seal with a pointed knife. Check the seasoning and serve hot.

Beef with Pears and Chestnuts

I remember travelling to Lérida in Spain many years ago to begin exploring the cooking of Catalonia. The drive had been rather hazardous and we arrived in the early autumn dusk feeling exhausted and disoriented. It was my first introduction to late dining. We were starving by 6.30 p.m., and by the time we eventually sat down to dinner at 10 p.m. I felt too tired to eat. I slumped rather listlessly until the first artichokes arrived to perk me up and by the time the main course arrived I felt like Lazarus. Every October, when I see the first chestnuts of the season, I recreate that marvellous beef stew from Lérida.

6 small pears
2.5 cm (1 in) cinnamon stick
2 teaspoons sugar
300 g (11 oz) chestnuts
1.5 kg (3 lb) lean beef
salt and freshly ground black pepper
4 tablespoons olive oil
200 ml (7 fl oz) dry white wine
2 cloves garlic, chopped
1 slice stale white bread, crusts removed
25 g (1 oz) blanched almonds
2 plum tomatoes, peeled and chopped

Wash the pears and stew whole with the cinnamon stick, sugar and a little water until soft. Slash the flat side of the chestnuts and cook in a little boiling water for about 25 minutes. Cut the beef into 1 cm ($\frac{1}{2}$ in) strips, season and brown them in a little hot olive oil. Remove them with a slotted spoon and place in a flameproof casserole with the wine and a little water. Stew gently on the top of the stove for $1\frac{1}{2}$ hours or until tender.

Fry the garlic and bread in the same oil used for the beef. Place them in a food processor, wipe out the pan and dry-roast the almonds. Add the almonds to the food processor and blend the bread, garlic and almonds together.

Heat the remaining olive oil in the pan and add the tomatoes. Let them cook for about 10 minutes while you peel the chestnuts. These will start to crumble as you remove the skins. Stir the bread, garlic and almond mixture into the tomatoes and season to taste. Process briefly to make a thick purée and stir in the large crumbs of chestnut.

Lift out the pears, remove the cores and cut into slices. Stir carefully into the tomato and chestnut mixture.

When the meat is cooked, combine all the ingredients and leave to stand for 30 minutes to allow the flavours to amalgamate. Re-heat gently and serve.

Olive Ripiene

STUFFED OLIVES

These unusual deep-fried olives make a lovely 'nibble' to go with pre-dinner drinks. They are a speciality from the Marche region on the Italian Adriatic coast, and every family has its favourite stuffing.

1 tablespoon lean minced (ground) meat
1 tablespoon freshly grated Parmesan cheese
2 eggs
$\frac{1}{4}$ teaspoon ground cinnamon
$\frac{1}{4}$ teaspoon ground nutmeg
salt and freshly ground black pepper
30 very large green queen olives, stoned
plain (all-purpose) white flour
breadcrumbs
olive oil for deep-frying
1 lemon, finely sliced

Make a fine paste with the meat, cheese and one of the eggs. Add the spices and season to taste. Fill the stoned olives with this mixture. Then roll the stuffed olives in flour, dip in beaten egg, and roll in breadcrumbs.

Heat the oil and deep-fry the olives at 180°C, 350°F, until golden brown. Serve hot, garnished with slices of lemon.

Braciole di Maiale alla Napoletana

ROLLED NEAPOLITAN PORK SLICES

In southern Italy meat used to be rather poor quality and very expensive. Traditional recipes tended to involve long, slow cooking to make the meat tender and produce a thick sauce which was used with pasta in order to economize and provide another meal. Involtini *means thin rolled slices of meat.*

50 g (2 oz) capers
100 g (4 oz) cured ham
25 g (1 oz) pine nuts
50 g (2 oz) sultanas (white raisins)
3 tablespoons breadcrumbs
6 thin slices pork
salt and freshly ground black pepper
3 tablespoons olive oil
2 tablespoons dry white wine
3 tablespoons fresh tomato sauce (see page 38)
1 hot chilli pepper

Rinse the capers and dry on a paper towel. Chop the ham, nuts and sultanas and mix together with the breadcrumbs and capers. Beat the slices of pork until they are very thin, then season and arrange the breadcrumb mixture on each slice. Roll up and fasten with a toothpick or wind a little fine thread round each roll.

Heat the oil and gently brown the pork rolls all over. Pour over the wine, stir in the tomato sauce and add the chilli pepper. Cover and cook very slowly for about 2 hours. Lift out the pork rolls, remove the fastening and serve each one with a spoonful of sauce.

Stracotto al Marsala

BRAISED VEAL IN MARSALA WINE

Marsala, on the western coast of Sicily, just below Trapani, was virtually unknown to the rest of Europe until 1773, when a storm at sea forced the English merchant John Woodhouse to put into shore. He liked the local wine and thought it compared favourably with Port and Madeira. With consummate skill he managed to fix a very good price and establish a monopoly. By 1800 the wine was so firmly established with the English that Horatio Nelson described it as 'manna', and ordered huge supplies for his officers. The local people at Marsala enjoyed their good fortune at the hands of the mad English, and were philosophical about giving up their wine for foreign consumption. As a result, recipes such as this one using Marsala are comparatively recent.

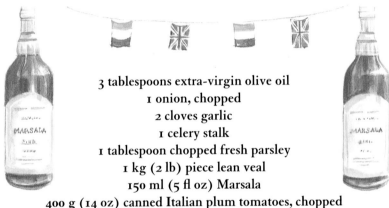

3 tablespoons extra-virgin olive oil
1 onion, chopped
2 cloves garlic
1 celery stalk
1 tablespoon chopped fresh parsley
1 kg (2 lb) piece lean veal
150 ml (5 fl oz) Marsala
400 g (14 oz) canned Italian plum tomatoes, chopped
2 carrots, sliced
2 courgettes (zucchini), sliced
1 aubergine (eggplant), sliced
1 large potato, chopped
6 fresh basil leaves
salt and freshly ground black pepper
450 ml (15 fl oz) stock

Heat the oil and gently fry the onion, garlic, celery and parsley. When the mixture begins to change colour, put in the meat, turning it around so that each side is gently browned. Moisten with a little Marsala each time you turn the meat. After 20 minutes add the tomatoes, the vegetables and basil. Season, cover and stew slowly for 2 hours, adding only enough stock to have a dense, thick sauce. Cut into thick slices and serve.

Habas alla Catalana

BROAD BEANS WITH SAUSAGES AND MINT

Many Spanish dishes include broad (fava) beans among the ingredients and livestock breeders even feed them to bulls before a fight to give the animals extra energy and stamina! I love this recipe which combines the beans with sausages and mint. There are also variations which omit the mint and substitute bacon or ham for the sausages.

500 g (1 lb 2 oz) pork sausages
2 tablespoons olive oil
100 g (4 oz) streaky (sliced) bacon, diced
1 large onion, finely chopped
2 cloves garlic, finely chopped
1 kg (2 lb) shelled broad (fava) beans
salt and freshly ground black pepper
6 tablespoons dry white wine
1 tablespoon chopped fresh mint

Prick the sausages so that the fat can run out, place in a large saucepan and cover with cold water. Bring to the boil and boil for 10 minutes. Remove the sausages from the pan and cut into 1 cm ($\frac{1}{2}$ in) slices.

Heat the oil and fry the bacon until crisp. Remove with a slotted spoon, drain on a paper towel and reserve. Gently cook the onion and garlic until they begin to change colour. Meanwhile boil the beans in salted water for 10 minutes or until cooked. Drain, and reserve the cooking liquid.

Pour the wine and about 150 ml (5 fl oz) of reserved bean cooking water into the garlic and onion mixture, then add the sausage, bacon and mint. Stir well and cook gently for 15 minutes. Add the cooked beans, black pepper and check the salt. Serve in a terracotta bowl if possible.

Meatballs and Courgettes

In the past a less expensive ingredient was often combined with meat to make it more economical. This Turkish recipe combines courgettes (zucchini) with meat, but aubergines (eggplants) or artichoke hearts are found in other countries' variations. Today, when many people do not have a vegetable garden, meat may be the less costly ingredient, but it is healthy to reduce the amount of meat, and some very interesting flavours and textures can be achieved with these meat and vegetable mixtures.

4 tablespoons olive oil
1 large onion, chopped
500 g (1 lb 2 oz) courgettes (zucchini) or marrow, sliced
500 g (1 lb 2 oz) lean minced (ground) lamb, veal or beef
1 egg, beaten
50 g (2 oz) hard cheese (e.g. Parmesan or Cheddar), grated
salt and freshly ground black pepper
flour for dredging

Heat 1 tablespoon of the oil and gently fry the onion. Cook the courgettes in boiling, salted water until soft. Drain well and press out all the water. In a food processor grind the meat to a fine paste, then add the onion, courgettes, egg, cheese and seasoning. If the mixture seems too wet I leave it in a sieve to drain for about 30 minutes in the refrigerator. Roll the mixture into small walnut-sized balls and dredge with flour. Heat the remaining oil and fry the balls gently so that they cook evenly and become an attractive golden brown. Drain on paper towels.

DESSERTS

MEDITERRANEAN
fruit ripened in the warm breezes coming inland from
the sea, or down from the hills, has a very special flavour,
and a bowl of fresh seasonal fruit makes the perfect
ending to a meal. At times this is expanded to include a
selection of dried fruit and nuts, or the fruits appear as a
delicate sorbet or jelly. There is no rich pasture land to
supply cream or butter, so these ingredients play no part
in traditional Mediterranean meals.

The Arab influence has produced sweet cakes and
biscuits made with honey, nuts and dried fruits, but many
of these need to be prepared by a professional pastry
maker, and they are usually too sweet to serve at the end
of a meal. In this part of the world hospitality is legendary,
and these sweets are usually kept to serve to visitors, with
a glass of wine, tea or coffee, depending on local custom.

In southern Spain many desserts use the egg yolks that
were left over after the whites had been employed in the
production of sherry, and in Italy Ricotta cheese appears
in many sweet guises. Greece and Turkey have many
honey pastries and every country uses the fragrant citrus
fruits to make refreshing desserts.

In the following selection I have gathered together
some interesting 'new' recipes that are made with
traditional ingredients used to create the light desserts
that are so pleasing to modern tastes.

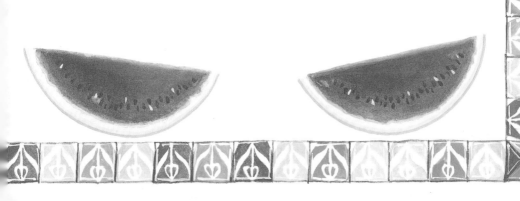

Glace à la Lavande

LAVENDER ICE-CREAM

In Provence whole fields are filled with great purple strips of lavender, and I had always assumed that the flowers were grown for the perfume factories around Grasse, and that the fragrant lavender honey was a happy by-product from local bees. Then I visited Roger Vergé's restaurant 'Moulin', at Mougins, tasted his delectable lavender ice-cream, and realized that the Provençal cuisine has learned to imitate the bees and to savour these lovely flowers to the full. It is essential to use fresh lavender or packets of lavender sugar, if available, because dried lavender has often been produced for bath preparations and contains additional non-edible perfume essence.

1 tablespoon lavender flowers, washed and dried
200 g (7 oz) sugar
250 ml (8 fl oz) milk
8 egg yolks
250 ml (8 fl oz) crème fraîche
6 fresh lavender sprigs
extra sugar, powdered in a food processor

In a food processor combine the washed and dried flowers with the sugar to make a lavender powder. Dissolve this sugar in the milk. Stir the yolks into the crème fraîche and mix the milk and crème fraîche together. Pour this mixture into an ice-cream machine, following the instructions in the usual way.

If you do not have an ice-cream maker, freeze the cooled milk and crème fraîche mixture. Remove from the freezer, place in a food processor and blend until it is frothy. Return to the freezer. Transfer to the refrigerator about an hour before serving. Wash the lavender sprigs, roll in powdered sugar and leave to dry on a plate lightly covered with sugar. Serve the ice-cream in lozenge-shaped portions, shaped by two spoons dipped in boiling water. Decorate with the lavender sprigs.

Semifreddo di Torrone in Crema di Pistacchi

NOUGAT PUDDING WITH PISTACHIO SAUCE

Cremona is justly famous for its delicious nougat, and no Italian Christmas would be complete without great white bars of torrone. This recipe uses the traditional nougat and amaretti biscuits to make an unusual dessert.

200 g (7 oz) white nougat
100 g (4 oz) amaretti biscuits
4 eggs, separated
150 g (5 oz) sugar
3 tablespoons brandy
500 ml (17 fl oz) cream, whipped

Sauce
100 g (4 oz) shelled and peeled pistachio nuts
2 egg yolks
75 g (3 oz) sugar
250 ml (8 fl oz) milk

Chop the nougat into very small pieces and reduce the amaretti to coarse crumbs. Beat together the egg yolks and sugar until they are light and creamy. Whip the egg whites until they are stiff. Stir the brandy into the yolks, then carefully fold in the egg whites. Gently add the nougat and amaretti and the whipped cream. Turn into a mould and put in the freezer for several hours.

Put a few pistachio nuts to one side for decoration. Chop the remaining nuts very finely. Beat together the yolks and sugar for the sauce, then stir in the nuts. Bring the milk to the boil and slowly pour it into the egg mixture, stirring continuously. Return to the heat and simmer slowly, stirring until the mixture thickens and starts to coat the back of the spoon. Leave to cool, then sieve the sauce.

Transfer the nougat pudding from the freezer to the refrigerator an hour before serving. Turn out the pudding, divide into portions, and serve each one with a spoonful of sauce and a few slivers of pistachio nuts scattered on top.

Harem Navels

These biscuits used to be cooked in the vast kitchens of Topkapi Palace, Istanbul. Many Turkish dishes pay homage to beautiful women and remind us of the expression 'Looks good enough to eat'. The plump, soft, oval meatballs seductively called 'Ladies' thighs' always make me feel better about my 'rounded' limbs, and these small lightly-tanned rings evoke the allure of belly-dancers.

200 g (7 oz) sugar
1 tablespoon lemon juice
50 g (2 oz) butter
75 g (3 oz) plain (all-purpose) white flour
1 teaspoon salt
1 egg plus 1 yolk
olive oil for deep-frying

Dissolve the sugar in 250 ml (8 fl oz) water and bring to the boil. Simmer for 10 minutes, then add the lemon juice. Simmer for another 5 minutes, then allow to cool. Reserve this sugar syrup.

Melt the butter over a low heat and pour in 225 ml ($7\frac{1}{2}$ fl oz) water. Bring back to the boil, add the flour and salt and stir continuously with a wooden spoon. Keep stirring until the mixture begins to leave the sides of the pan, then remove the pan from the heat. Let the mixture cool a little, then gradually beat in the whole egg and then the extra yolk. I usually use my hand electric mixer to do this.

Put some oil on your hands and form small balls with the mixture, then flatten them to make 3 cm ($1\frac{1}{4}$ in) diameter discs. Poke your finger through the middle to make a hole. Heat the oil until it is lukewarm: 130°C, 250°F. Do not let it get too hot because the dough will not rise. Deep-fry a few biscuits at a time and as they swell and float to the top increase the temperature slightly. When they are golden brown all over, remove with a slotted spoon and drain on paper towels.

When they are cool, drop them into the sugar syrup. They will get sweeter the longer they are left in the syrup. I usually remove them after 5 minutes.

Flan de Naranja

ORANGE CUSTARD

All over Spain there are variations of this lovely light dessert. It can be served hot or cold, but I like to serve it cold, from individual dariole moulds.

150 g (5 oz) sugar
6 egg yolks
juice 6 oranges
6 oranges

Pre-heat the oven to 180°C, 350°F (Gas Mark 4).

Beat together the sugar and yolks until they are thick and creamy. Stir in the unfiltered orange juice, then pour the mixture into dariole moulds that have been rinsed in cold water. Put the moulds into a baking tin, pouring in enough boiling water to come half-way up the sides of the moulds and bake for an hour. Allow to cool, then place in the refrigerator.

Peel the oranges, removing all the white skin, and with a serrated knife cut into thin rounds. Turn out each custard onto the middle of a small plate, and arrange one orange per serving in overlapping rings round it.

Ricotta Soufflé

This is a 'new' recipe from the south of Italy using traditional ingredients like Ricotta cheese and citrus fruits, in an original way.

300 g (11 oz) Ricotta cheese
3 eggs, separated
100 g (4 oz) candied citrus peel, preferably mandarin
50 g (2 oz) sugar plus extra to taste
juice of 6 mandarins or 3 oranges

Put the Ricotta cheese in a strainer and leave for at least 1 hour to drain off the excess liquid.

Pre-heat the oven to 180°C, 350°F (Gas Mark 4).

Beat the eggs yolks into the Ricotta cheese. Stir in the candied peel and a little sugar. The mixture should not be too sweet because it will be served with orange sauce.

Heat 50 g (2 oz) sugar and the juice, stirring until the sugar dissolves. Then reserve two-thirds of the mixture to serve with the cooked dessert. The remaining syrup should be boiled quickly and the resulting caramel swirled round individual ramekin dishes to coat the surface.

Whip the egg whites until stiff and fold into the Ricotta mixture. Spoon into the ramekin dishes, cover with buttered foil and cook by standing the ramekins in a pan of boiling water over a gentle flame as in a *bain marie*. After 15 minutes remove the ramekins, brown the surface of the soufflés under a hot grill (broiler) and serve with the warm fruit syrup.

Campari and Grapefruit Sorbet

This delicious sorbet recipe was given to me by pastry chef Robert Coco, who was born in Sicily of Italian parents, but now lives in Australia.

175 g (6 oz) sugar
200 ml (7 fl oz) grapefruit juice
3 tablespoons Campari
250 ml (8 fl oz) white wine
dash of grenadine
juice of 1 large lemon

Bring 200 ml (7 fl oz) water and the sugar to the boil and let the sugar dissolve. Remove the pan from the heat, add the rest of the ingredients, mix well and pour through a fine strainer. Let the mixture cool, then freeze in an ice-cream machine, if you have one, or in a container in the coldest part of the freezer, stirring once or twice during the freezing process to prevent ice crystals forming.

I like to serve this slightly bitter sorbet as a refreshing dessert at the end of an elaborate meal, accompanied by the Turkish Harem Navels (see page 118).

Crema e Granita al Caffé

ESPRESSO COFFEE CUSTARDS WITH COFFEE GRANITA

To make this dessert, it is essential to have an Italian espresso coffee pot and you need Italian roast coffee to get the full flavour. It is now possible to get vacuum-packed Italian coffee which will work very well, but do make very strong coffee, packing down the coffee with the back of a spoon.

Granita
250 g (9 oz) sugar
500 ml (17 fl oz) strong espresso coffee

Custard
3 eggs plus 3 yolks
3 tablespoons sugar
200 ml (7 fl oz) cream
150 ml (5 fl oz) strong espresso coffee

Pre-heat the oven to 180°C, 350°F (Gas Mark 4).

To make the granita bring 250 ml (8 fl oz) water to the boil with the sugar, stirring until the sugar dissolves. Let the mixture boil over a moderate heat for 5 minutes. Remove from the heat, stir in the coffee, and when the mixture has cooled pour into ice-cube trays and place in the freezer.

To make the custard beat together the eggs, yolks and sugar until light and creamy. Stir the cream into the coffee and heat without letting the mixture boil. Pour through a strainer onto the eggs, stirring all the time. Pour into six dariole moulds, which have been rinsed in cold water and not dried. Stand the moulds in a baking tin, pour in enough boiling water to come half-way up the moulds and cook in the oven for about 25 minutes. Remove from the oven and allow to cool before placing in the refrigerator for at least 6 hours.

When ready to serve, turn out on a flat plate. Remove the iced coffee from the freezer and chop in a food processor to make coarse crystals. Arrange in a heap around the coffee custards. Serve at once.

Pastry Filled with Nuts and Honey

I don't know the origin of this delicious dish, but it has a North African flavour. The triangles are very sweet, so I usually serve one for each person at the end of the meal with strong espresso coffee.

3 sheets filo pastry
50 g (2 oz) shelled hazelnuts
50 g (2 oz) shelled pistachio nuts
3 tablespoons honey (lavender or thyme)
6 tablespoons olive oil
oil for deep-frying

Chop all the nuts until they resemble coarse breadcrumbs, then stir in the honey. Place the sheets of filo pastry one on top of another, and cut into 6 rectangles about 6 cm ($2\frac{1}{2}$ in) wide and 36 cm (14 in) long. Using a pastry brush, coat the first filo pastry strip with olive oil. Put another strip on top and coat this in the same way. Arrange a third strip on top and place a little filling near one end, about 2 cm ($\frac{3}{4}$ in) in from the edge. Fold one corner over the filling, creating a triangle, and continue to fold it over on itself until the whole strip is folded up. Prepare all the strips in this way. Heat the oil to 180°C, 350°F, and deep-fry the triangles in batches until golden brown. Drain on paper towels and serve hot.

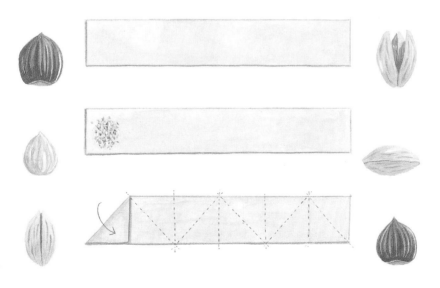

Pesche Ripiene

STUFFED PEACHES

This is an easy dessert, usually made at the height of summer with large white peaches. It is important to use ripe, firm fruit that has not been bruised, but any less perfect fruit can always be turned into frothy glasses of Bellini the delicious aperitivo made with champagne and fresh peach juice.

6 large peaches
6 macaroons, crushed
2 eggs
2 tablespoons sugar
60 g (2½ oz) unsalted butter, softened

Pre-heat the oven to 190°C, 375°F (Gas Mark 5).

Blanch the peaches in boiling water, one at a time, for half a minute. Remove with a slotted spoon and plunge into cold water so that it is easy to peel off the skin. Cut the peaches in half and remove the stone, then enlarge the hollow so that it will hold a large spoonful of filling. To make the filling chop the pulp you have removed and mix it together with the crushed macaroons, eggs, sugar and softened butter. Stuff the peach halves with this mixture and arrange them on a buttered ovenproof plate. Bake for about 20 minutes, basting from time to time with their cooking liquid.

This dish can be served hot or cold.

INDEX

atlantic ocean
FRANCE
SPAIN
MEDITERRANEAN
MOROCCO
ALGERIA
TUNISIA